THE
YELVERTON TO PRINCETOWN
RAILWAY

by
Anthony R. Kingdom

FOREST PUBLISHING
(In association with ARK Publications)

First published in 1991 by FOREST PUBLISHING
(in association with ARK Publications), Woodstock, Liverton, Newton
Abbot, Devon TQ12 6JJ

Copyright © Anthony R. Kingdom 1991

British Library Cataloguing in Publication Data
Kindom, Anthony R.
The Yelverton to Princetown Railway
I. Title
625.261094235

ISBN 0-9515274-3-6

2-6-2T No 4410 pulls away from Burrator & Sheepstor Halt with the 3.2 p.m.
train for Princetown on a cold spring day in 1953. The R.A.F. mast at Sharpitor
is clearly visible in the clear crisp air, whilst the waters of the lake look cold and
uninviting behind the dam below.   *Western Morning News*

FOREST PUBLISHING (In assocation with ARK Publications)
Editorial and design by: Mike and Roger Lang

Typeset by: Exe Valley Dataset Ltd, Exeter
Printed and bound in Great Britain by: BPC   Wheatons Ltd, Exeter

Cover photographs:
Front — *(Top)* 2-6-2T No. 4568 stands ready to leave Yelverton with the 1.22 p.m. (Saturdays
only) service to Princetown on 31st December 1955.   *Peter W. Gray*
(Lower) 2-6-2T No. 4410 heads the 12.8 p.m. train out of Princetown on a crisp but sunny
winter's day during the early 1950's.   *Western Morning News*

Back — 2-6-2T No. 4410 enters the outskirts of Princetown with the 2.51 p.m. ex Yelverton train
during the early 1950's. In the foreground can be seen Leedon Tor above the coach and Sharpitor,
with its R.A.F. mast against the skyline.   *Western Morning News*

FOREWORD

I am happy to write a foreword to Mr. Kingdom's 'History of the Princetown Railway', especially since much of the land it traversed belonged to my family.

There can be few short stretches of country which can equal this in beauty and variation of scenery. The line after leaving Yelverton and passing through Dousland, emerged on to Dartmoor, winding its way round Foggintor to Princetown.

My Grandfather often drove his carriage and pair from Maristow to catch the train, putting up his horses at the stables adjacent to the Station Master's house. A leisurely way of travelling no doubt, and far more relaxing than competing with crowded motorways and the difficulties of parking in modern times.

It was a great pity that this line could not have been kept open by some private Company, but the upkeep no doubt would have proved too expensive.

Many people, including my family, gathered together to ride on this train the day before the line closed and we all bemoaned its passing, but we had done very little before that to justify its retention.

Now it has passed into history and I have no doubt it will be faithfully recorded in the pages that follow, and remain of great interest to many people.

ROBOROUGH

BIBLIOGRAPHY

Go Great Western by T. W. Roche M.A. (Branch line Handbooks)
Great Western Engines Vol. 2 by J. H. Russell. (O.P.C.)
Great Western Engines, Names, Numbers & Classes, 1940 — Preservation by B. Whitehurst. (O.P.C.)
Historical Survey of Great Western Engine Sheds by E. Lyons C.Eng., M.I.Struc.E. (O.P.C.)
History of the Great Western Railway by E. T. MacDermot. (Ian Allan)
Locomotives of the GWR, parts 3, 5, 6 & 9. (R.C.T.S.)
Plymouth & Launceston by T. W. E. Roche M.A. (Branch Line Handbooks)
Regional History of the Railways of Great Britain by D. St J. Thomas. (David & Charles)
The Lee Moor Tramway by R. M. S. Hall. (Oakwood Press)
The Plymouth & Dartmoor Railway by H. G. Kendall. (Oakwood Press)
The Tavistock, Launceston & Princetown Railways by G. H. Anthony M.C.I.T. (Oakwood Press)
Through Western Windows by A. S. Caswell & T. W. E. Roche. (Town & Country Press)
Track Layout Diagrams of the GWR/BR (WR) by R. A. Cooke.

ACKNOWLEDGEMENTS

The author extends his sincere thanks to the following for their assistance, courtesy and time, given in all manner of ways during the preparation of this book.

Special thanks are due to Mr G. H. Anthony, M.C.I.T., the last Station Master of Plymouth, North Road, and author of *The Tavistock, Launceston & Princetown Railways* for his help and experience which lessened the burden of research considerably. Mr E. T. Anstead, A.R.I.B.A., for the loan of maps on the proposed Merivale Railway, together with much information on the two railways. Col C. R. Spencer of Elfordtown, Yelverton, for permission to photograph on the site of the old station at Yelverton. Mr E. J. Thomas, former signalman at Yelverton who has been the mainstay of information from local railway sources. Philip Powell of Croydon for his exhaustive research on my behalf at the Public Records Office, Kew. Brian Kohring and Mike Wyatt for the loan of the tickets from the branch. B. Gibson for the provision of Omnibus timetables so painstakingly compiled. L. Crozier for the historical Engineering and operating data notes. Roy Taylor for his superb map on page 56. Photographs are acknowledged individually except those taken by the author or from his private collection.

1. British Rail, Western Region.
2. Devon County Records Office, Exeter.
3. Great Western Society Ltd.
4. Ordnance Survey Office.
5. Plymouth City Library.
6. Plymouth & Devonport Weekly Journal (issue of 29th Oct. 1840).
7. Plymouth Railway Circle.
8. Public Records Office.
9. Signalling Records Society.
10. Tavistock Gazette (issue of 17th Feb. 1928).
11. Western Evening Herald. ⎤
12. Western Independent. ⎬ Various copies
13. Western Morning News. ⎦

E. T. Anstead; G. H. Anthony; J. Brokenshire; A. C. Clothier; M. Dickenson; C. Fennamore; C. Judge; W. Knott; B. Kohring; H. Pitts; P. Powell; Miss H. G. Q. Rowett; R. C. Sambourne; Col C. R. Spencer; R. E. Taylor; S. Taylor; E. J. Thomas; V. Thompson; C. Winsor; M. Wyatt.

PREFACE

"The Yelverton to Princetown Railway" is a virtual reprint of the original publication, "The Princetown Branch", published by the Oxford Publishing Company in 1979 as one of a popular series of branchline histories produced by that company before its subsequent change of ownership.

As a result of that change, the series found itself a "casualty of rationalisation" and reprints of existing books, together with any new ones, sadly, have long since ceased in their original format. However, with the copyright of the series since returned to the respective authors, I was able to re-present the manuscript of the Princetown Railway to its new publisher: most of the book remains the same although some photographs have changed, mainly for technical or copyright reasons.

Since the original publication, little has changed over most of the old track-bed for, of course, it runs over open moorland of the Dartmoor National Park. Indeed, about the only noticeable changes are at Dousland, where further building has encroached upon what remained of the line, particularly near the site of the level crossing: this has been completely obliterated and is now marked only by the former Crossing Keeper's Cottage, which, in its turn, has been modernised and extended into a desirable residence. In addition, further down the line at Prowse's Crossing, the Dousland Stores & Post Office (page 155) has since closed and this building, too, has been modernised and extended into another desirable dwelling.

Elsewhere nothing has altered apart from minor earthworks having been carried out, such as the removal of embankments and bridge, or underpass, abutments by farmers in order to permit easier and safer access to their farms. Even at Princetown the station site remains much the same as it was in 1979.

As an interesting aside, new material could well have evolved during the early 1980's when local Councillors and business people in and around the Princetown area conceived a scheme to lay a narrow gauge railway from the old terminus out as far as King Tor. This was to have been opened to the public, but with the particular interests of the sick, disabled and under-privileged children in mind. It was envisaged that holidays and casual visits by these children would allow them the opportunity of seeing the more remote parts of the moor which, hitherto, other forms of transport had denied them. Furthermore, even greater penetration of the moor could have been achieved by pony trekking and horse-riding facilities connecting with the halts.

Originally the Dartmoor Preservation Association Committee objected to the scheme on the grounds that the moor would be desecrated by heavy concentrations of visitors at particular locations, but this objection was later withdrawn, after further consideration had allayed these fears. There had, after all, been railways in the area from 1824 until 1956 without any desecration! However, after being invited to advise the scheme's committee on gauge, types of locomotive and rolling stock etc. in my capacity as the author of the line's history, and because of my knowledge of local railways, the scheme sadly came to nothing and an opportunity to bring new life into Princetown's economy was lost. Apparently one of the main stumbling blocks concerned the fencing of the line: this was necessary for reasons of safety but legally couldn't be done because it was on common land. Whatever, following my preliminary meeting with the committee's Lady Chairman, I heard no more on the subject and can only conclude that another reason for the scheme's failure was that the promised financial backing was either insufficient or not forthcoming.

Perhaps even during these times of recession, the idea could be resurrected? I am sure that such worthy bodies as 'Mencap' and 'Riding for the Disabled' would welcome such a project and give their organisations' influential backing to it. But for now I must be content with the fact that another chance has been given to me to publish the efforts of my pen to bring to the attentions of future generations the windswept beauty of this unique and lovely moorland line.

Anthony R. Kingdom
Thalassa
Newton Ferrers
Devon
June 1991

INTRODUCTION

The Princetown Branch was best known for its moorland scenery but was also known for its lack of profitability. A line from Plymouth to Princetown was first conceived as far back as 1818 with the object of opening up Dartmoor. The Plymouth & Dartmoor Railway to Kings Tor opened in 1823 and subsequent completion to Princetown followed by 1825. Granite and minerals formed the traffic down from the moor whilst coal, lime, timber and prison stores formed the upward traffic. Following its decline, which eventually left only the southern section as an outlet for the china clay traffic from Lee Moor, the section from Yelverton to Princetown was replaced by the Princetown Railway in 1883. It was worked by the Great Western Railway from its opening but did not become part of the GWR until as late as 1922. Before the construction of Yelverton station in 1885, trains ran to and from Horrabridge on the Plymouth to Launceston railway, itself a branch line.

Ten and a half miles was the distance taken for the line to negotiate the rugged tors lying between the two towns of Yelverton and Princetown which are only six miles apart, as the crow flies. During the journey which at the least, was spectacular and at the most, unique, passengers were elevated some 950 feet above the junction at Yelverton to be set down 1,373 feet above sea level at the terminus, Princetown, the highest station in England. The ruling gradient on the line was 1 in 40 and its sinuous course followed that of its predecessor almost completely.

The line always struggled for its existence in the sparsely populated area which it served. On the closure of the granite quarries in the early 1920s, the GWR, in an endeavour to stimulate passenger traffic to compensate the loss of freight, opened halts at Burrator and King Tor. Another at Ingra Tor followed in 1936. Their intention was that the halts should attract the moorland hiker and family picnic groups. Passengers in the main were schoolchildren and commuters to Tavistock and Plymouth. In addition there were the distinctly unusual passengers shackled to their warders, convicts travelling to and from the prison. In high summer, the hikers, picnickers and general holidaymakers came in their numbers to augment the regulars, their ranks sometimes swelled by families of the prisoners visiting their relatives.

During severe winters, long before the advent of the helicopter, a train was the only link with the outside world. Roads were the first casualties of heavy falling snows in this part of Devon. Freight, not passengers was the main concern during the freezing winter months. Food for the town, prison and the moorland cattle and sheep were the first consideration with fuel for heating a close second.

The increasing costs of operation, isolation and the old story of road motor competition spelled out redundancy long before the Beeching axe. The first signs of impending doom were obvious as early as 1954. After much protestation by various objecting bodies, closure came in March 1956. The final day passed in sombre curiosity and scant celebration by the hundreds that made the pilgrimage. So ended 73 years of history of the line together with no less than 133 years of Princetown railway history. Local newspapers carried full columns and pictures of the closure. The nationals too reported the events, *The Daily Telegraph* carried no less than 4 column inches on this, as yet uncommon event.

With its preponderance of panoramic views of Dartmoor, not only during familiar high summer, but also during the serene beauty of the freezing white bleakness of winter what better candidate to become a privately run steam railway, than this exquisitely beautiful moorland line? Sadly this line closed 22 years ago, and it is this very span of time that has robbed it of becoming one of the major attractions of railway preservation history. In 1956, funds were to be raised to purchase the line for such a private venture but suffered from lack of response. People at that point in time had suffered little from the loss of their railways. Education to this way of thinking was not to emerge for several years and even then it was with much effort that preservation and private ownership caught on.

One might well consider the fact, that with more closures still taking place to date, the track still being sold off, the majority of the trackbed of the Princetown line remains intact between Peek Hill and Princetown. There is yet still time if only sufficient funds could be raised!

Anthony R. Kingdom
June 1979

Yelverton station looking towards Plymouth during the early 1900's. A down train to Tavistock receives the 'right away' on the 'main' line whilst the rear of the Princetown train is seen waiting in the bay. Note the early track layout.
Lens of Sutton

Two views of Horrabridge station, former junction for Princetown until the opening of Yelverton station in 1885. a) Looking towards Yelverton, b) Looking towards Tavistock.

Author's collection.

a small spur backwards on the eastern side whilst at the far end there was a turn out into a facing spur on the southern end. This siding was equipped with reversing facilities onto the turntable road and inspection pit. The turntable was provided not to turn the engine, but for turning the snow-plough during winter! The engine generally returned from Princetown bunker first and the method for changing ends at Yelverton was by a 'run around employing gravity procedure'. This will be described in full in the Branch Working chapter.

One is very tempted at this juncture to describe a journey on the branch during the halcyon days of the 1920s, but to describe a journey during the twilight years of the early 1950s is, I feel, preferable. It will enable a greater number of people who read this book to enjoy happy and nostalgic memories of the line and it is to this end I direct my efforts.

A 44XX class Tank and two non-corridor coaches forming the branch train stand in their platform waiting for the off, after completing the 'running around the train' procedure on arrival. The branch 'down starter' standing at the end of the platform, a few feet from the engine, drops and gives the 'right away'. The train moves out of the station and commences a steep climb on a rising gradient of 1 in 40. Heading in a south easterly direction and immediately clearing the points into the turntable road and engine siding, the 'up home' signal guarding the approach to the station is passed, viewed from the rear. Here the first glimpses of line back to Plymouth are seen running south and shrouded on both sides by the sylvan cloak of Chubb Tor Wood. As the line continues on a curve towards the north east, m.p. ¼ and Yelverton's 'down advanced starter' are passed simultaneously with the crossing of an underpass. The scenery has already opened out at this point to green fields bordered at their foot by the river Meavy and backed by the Olderwood Plantation. Further to the south but obscured by trees is the little hamlet of Hoo Meavy. Northwards from this point lie the scattered and as yet distant environs of Yelverton, but Elfordtown, the home of Col Spencer, is more prominent in the distinctly rural scenery. The line having settled for a north easterly direction, continues on its embankment crossing two iron bridges south of Gratton Cross. The first, over the Yelverton to Cornwood road via Cadover Bridge, and the second, over the Yelverton to Meavy road. The embankment continues toward the ½ m.p. to the rear of Yelverton Park Villas to the east and Willowby Park and Willowby House to the west of the line. Away to the south east and just over a mile distant lies the village of Meavy with its 'Royal Oak' in which King Charles I was said to have hidden from the 'Roundheads'. After the ½ m.p. the embankment quickly gives way to a deepening cutting running below the eastern suburbs of Yelverton. At a point where Southella Road runs parallel to the line, the now disused Plymouth and Devonport leats cross the line by means of large iron aqueducts standing on granite legs. In addition a right of way into the fields on the eastern side of the line is provided for by a three arch granite overbridge. These aqueducts were initially installed to carry the water from the leats over the line during the construction of the railway

The three arch accommodation bridge and two aqueducts between M.P. ½ and M.P. ¾. The aqueducts carried the Plymouth and Devonport leats over the line and were demolished in 1960. This cutting is now completely filled in and only the parapets of the bridge are visible.   *S. Taylor*

Views of two bridges between Yelverton and Dousland. The top picture shows the lineside view of the bridge over the Yelverton to Cornwood road at Gratton Cross. The lower picture shows the bridge at Lake Lane, looking towards Woodman's Corner.

when their original course was impeded. With the cutting still deepening below the outer suburbs of Binkham and Little Binkham Hills, the Yelverton 'up fixed distant' and m.p. ¾ are passed to the right of the line.

Breaking out of the cutting and running on an embankment parallel to the B3212, Yelverton to Princetown road, some 130 yards away, the line takes a more easterly course crossing the Devonport leat by Leat Cottage. Here the line also crosses a small iron bridge carrying a road into the hamlet of Lake from the Princetown road at Woodmans Corner. The cross roads at Woodmans Corner, north east of the line, is where the roads to Walkhampton Lake and Binkham Farm break away from the B3212. The first varied views of the moor unfold as the line now runs parallel with the road, the Devonport leat to the north and the Plymouth leat to the south, passing Dousland 'down fixed distant' and the 1¼ m.p. Passing north of Merrifield and having debouched itself alongside the Princetown road, the line is protected from it by a high creosoted wooden fence. This was erected to prevent horses and ponies from being scared by the trains. The 1½ m.p. is then passed just prior to entering Dousland station at 1m. 47chs. from Yelverton. On entering Dousland station and passing through it, a plethora of signals are encountered. No less than seven signals are sighted, controlling a platform road, passing loop, two goods shed sidings and a level crossing. They were in order as follows:— the 'down home', the 'up starter', the 'down starter', the 'up inner home', and at the level crossing the pair of signals comprising of the 'down advance starter' and 'lower arm distant', the latter was slotted with and was operated by the ground frame at Prowses Crossing. The last signal was the 'up home' on the far side of the Dousland crossing (all 'down' signals were facing the train en route for Princetown and all 'up' signals showed the backs of their arms in this direction). The gate controls for the Dousland crossing were housed in a covered ground frame adjacent to the Dousland side of the crossing gates.

The station at Dousland was very picturesque and was built on a curve. It consisted of a platform on the down side constructed of stone filling faced with brick. The covering was of loose stone chippings edged with concrete slabs with rounded shoulders on the lineside. In later days a timber extension was erected at the western end. It was backed from the adjacent road by a sturdy high granite wall, at the eastern end of which stood a signal box and station building. The signal box replaced an earlier one which stood on the site of the crossing ground frame. It was a small box, toylike in appearance, its windows often filled with geraniums. It was built of granite with its rear wall forming part of the boundary wall, which made its height at platform level only 10 feet to the roof. Above the 10 feet mark it had a timber roof, apex in design and covered with slates, the ridges finished in zinc sheeting. All around vision of the line was provided by eight timber framed windows two of which on the ends of the box were of a sliding type. It had a 14 lever frame with only one spare lever and bore the unusual nameplate in cast iron of 'Dousland Barn Signal Box'.

16

A fine summer's day on 5th July 1955, with closure less than a year away. A solitary passenger makes for the exit of Dousland station as No 4410 and its coach pulls away towards the level crossing. *R.C. Riley*

Later the same day as No 4410 returns from Princetown with an additional coach. *R.C. Riley*

A train spotter winds on his camera after taking a 'shot' of an up train. The picture shows the timber extension to the platform at the western end of Dousland station. *Author's collection.*

A dramatic view of a mixed train entering Dousland station as viewed from the brake van during July 1955. *R.C. Riley*

rounded heights of Eylesbarrow. Since the second world war and until the late 1960s, there stood the steel lattice framework of the R.A.F. Sharpitor radio station. It served during those years as a most confusing landmark to railway travellers on the branch. The tortuous meanderings of the Princetown branch over and around the many tors, gave sightings of this mast first from one side of the train and then the other! It was called Sharpitor but in fact, it stood nearer to Peek Hill below it and could of course, be clearly seen from Burrator Halt.

Restarting from Burrator Halt, the close association with the Devonport leat is kept on the western side as m.p. 3 is passed. The line then ran into a belt of conifers planted as a water catchment and protection for the nearby reservoir. Here the Devonport leat ducks under the line and runs parallel to the eastern side behind Burrator Lodge at m.p. 3¾. Still travelling in a northerly direction, the line takes up close company with the minor road in from the B3212, Princetown road at Yennadon Cross. At the same time the Devonport leat swings away eastwards to the higher moor. Continuing its journey through the conifers, the 'down fixed distant' for Lowery Crossing is passed followed by m.p. 3½. Immediately afterwards the line emerges from the wood into a small clearing, as it runs on a shallow embankment crossing the accompanying minor road via a small iron bridge, before making its final approach to Lowery Crossing.

This lonely level crossing was attended by a resident keeper until approximately 1927 when it was down graded to an unmanned crossing fitted with warning bells, the ground frame was removed and the workable distant signals made fixed. The warning bells were worked by treadles which were operated by the approaching trains. However the crossing keeper's cottage survived the change in status and was let by the railway as a private residence for a number of years. The gates were always open to the railway once the crossing was unmanned and it was the responsibility of any motorist to open them to the roadway and proceed if no warning bells were audible, closing the same afterwards. At the time of our journey the train's approach was marked by the sighting of the former crossing keeper's cottage to the right of the line and by a platelayers hut to the left. They were closely followed by the crossing itself which carried a back road from Lowery Cross into the hamlet of Lowery. Lowery was a hamlet of deserted farms near the shores of Burrator lake to the east of the line.

Having successfully negotiated the crossing, the train continues its climb on a 1 in 41 gradient towards the open moor passing m.p. 3¾ almost immediately. Here the dense population of the conifer woods seem almost distant as the line enters a cutting before finally emerging onto the open moor. Suddenly the cutting gives way to an embankment and the train bursts out of the woods to give the first totally different views of Dartmoor. Running on a steepening embankment, the line crosses the B3212 by means of the granite Peek Hill bridge. The views from the bridge were varied and extensive to the north west, with the Walkham valley, backed by distant Pew Tor, (1050 feet above sea level), and the river Walkham flowing past the village of Walkhampton. Further towards the west, could be seen the larger village of Horrabridge,

Two views either side of Lowery Crossing on a bright day during the mid '50s, both showing 2-6-2T No 4410 and its coach.

The former on its way 'down' to Princetown, having just left the crossing on its way to Peek Hill. The latter returning 'up' from Princetown and seen just prior to entering the cutting before Lowery Crossing.   *R.C. Sambourne*

A mixed train negotiating the severe curve at M.P. 6., just prior to entering Ingra
Tor Halt. Photograph taken from the single coach on 15th June 1926.

H.C. Casserley

The loneliness of the moor is clearly shown in this fine view of Ingra Tor Halt on
5th July 1955. A mixed train can just be seen descending from Princetown in the
centre distance.

R.C. Riley

ticular, are views of vast areas of moor with Criptor as the predominant feature in the foreground. Nearer the railway, the old quarry workings dating back to Plymouth & Dartmoor Railway days, are still in existence in this little disturbed spot.

Ingra Tor Halt, like Burrator, is a platform wholly constructed of wood with a white painted shelter standing to its rear. The platform stood on wooden trestle legs and the fencing ran along its back edge passing the shelter which stood outside it. A small white gate led out onto the moor past the famous 'snake notice' and in so doing gave access to the door of the shelter on its eastern end. Two posts carrying lamp frames stood on the platform and provided illumination after dark. The guard on the 4.0 pm evening train ex Princetown, inserted oil wells into these and lit them whilst the guard of the 7.0 pm ex Yelverton (or last train) extinguished them and recovered them for filling and returning the following evening.

Leaving Ingra Tor Halt, the train continues across Walkhampton Common in an easterly direction and prepares to make a wide sweep around the declivity known as Yes Tor bottom. Passing m.p. 6½, followed soon afterwards by a platelayers hut, the train passes under a small granite bridge as it moves across an embankment and runs north easterly past m.p. 6¾. Turning in a tight curve to the east of Yes Tor Farm, the train negotiates a further embankment which contains a large culvert to allow an otherwise impeded stream to pass under it. Quickly following this the line twists around, through a shallow cutting to the north west and past m.p. 7 with its accompanying platelayers hut.

It is at m.p. 7 that m.p.9 lies only half a mile across the moor but 200 feet above it in a north easterly direction! The two points are connected by a grass road which runs to Foggintor via King Tor Halt, the next stop. This road turns into a track as it passes through the quarries and eventually emerges on to the Princetown to Tavistock road west of Rendlestone. Leaving m.p. 7, the train winds its way past the north east of Criptor towards m.p. 7¼, having now veered into a north westerly direction. After m.p. 7¼ the line runs along the slopes of Kings Tor below the extensive but disused workings of Swelltor Quarries. Keeping in a north easterly direction past a platelayers hut, some 100 yards short of the 7½ m.p. the train heads for Swelltor sidings at m.p. 7¾. Here was the junction to Swelltor Quarry, known as Royal Oak siding which was controlled by a ground frame, whose isolated yellow box could be clearly spotted from far across the moor. Although at the time of this journey the quarry was disused, the sidings are still in evidence. A forward siding ran off the running line in the 'down' direction with a much longer reverse siding running back into the quarry. A passing loop was also provided on the reverse siding.

Continuing from Swelltor sidings, the train passes over a granite overbridge and squeals around a tight curve past m.p. 8 and another platelayers hut standing at the end of a short embankment. Heading under the very rocks of Kings Tor, the view offered to passengers on a clear day was of a completely different vista again. Dominated by the

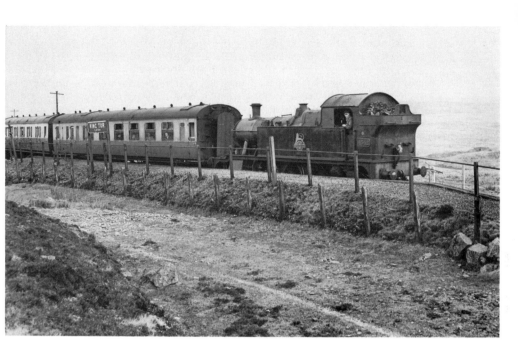

Two fine views of the 2.17 p.m. train for Yelverton at King Tor Platform, and a few moments after leaving, on a summer's day in 1955.   *Western Morning News*

mighty Great Mis Tor (1760 ft above sea level) and with Merrivale
Stone Rows visible in the foreground, the much smaller Hucken Tor
and Longash Farm resided nearer the track. Continuing on the tight
curve, the line veers east, passes m.p. 8¼ and veers south east again.
With the Merrivale Stone Rows behind it, the train passes two more
platelayers huts, the latter at m.p. 8½ as it makes its approach to the
next Halt at King Tor. The final run to King Tor Halt passes m.p. 8¾
and gives clear views of the trackbeds of former sidings, into the quarries
to the north east at Foggintor and south west at Swelltor. Now used as
cart tracks or footpaths across the moorland wastes, they actually
crossed the Princetown line by means of a level crossing near the halt.

King Tor Halt was constructed as a gravel topped earthworks
finished and edged at the lineside with timber. Fencing ran along the
back of the platform and the usual two lamp posts stood, one either end
and devoid of oil wells during daytime. The halt was also equipped with
a very large nameboard and a seat much weathered by the elements.
One side of the level crossing to the south eastern end of the platform,
stood the customary wooden shelter whilst at the other end stood
another platelayers hut. The views from the halt were once again, quite
different. Looking down to the west and the line below, one could
clearly see nearby Ingra Tor with Leeden Tor, Sheepstor, Leather Tor
and Eylesbarrow in the distance with the far distant gleam of Plymouth
Sound on the horizon. In the opposite direction could be seen rounded
southern slopes of Hessary Tor and Princetown itself.

Leaving King Tor Halt the train heads south east, past m.p. 9 with
the footpath running along the right hand side of the line. Turning to
due east and passing an old ruin, the line again alters course to the
north east as it passes m.p. 9¼ with an accompanying platelayers hut.
Soon afterwards an embankment is encountered which continues over
an underpass before being replaced by a cutting in which the 9½ m.p. is
passed. Emerging from the cutting past a platelayers hut and m.p. 9¾,
passengers can now see their motor bound counterparts moving to and
from Princetown along the B3212 road to the south of the line. It is
here the final run into Princetown is commenced. By m.p. 10 the road
is running parallel to the line as the train approaches the 'down fixed
distant' for Princetown. Two small embankments follow, the first is
bisected by a granite bridge over a stream running down to nearby old
tin workings, and subsequently joining with the first trickles of the river
Meavy.

At m.p. 10¼ the adjoining road has drawn that much nearer but
finally runs parallel again to the line as it approaches the station.
Following m.p. 10¼, the Princetown 'down home' is passed just prior
to the pointwork for the loop. Here also a steel bridge, mounted on
granite abutments and flanked by two rising embankments, spans the
line with a cart track and footpath. The track came in from near the old
toll houses on the B3212 to the old mine workings to the north of the
line. As the train enters the station under the bridge, it passes the rear
of the 'up starter' on its left whilst on its right further pointwork off
the loop provided access to sidings into the goods shed, loco shed and

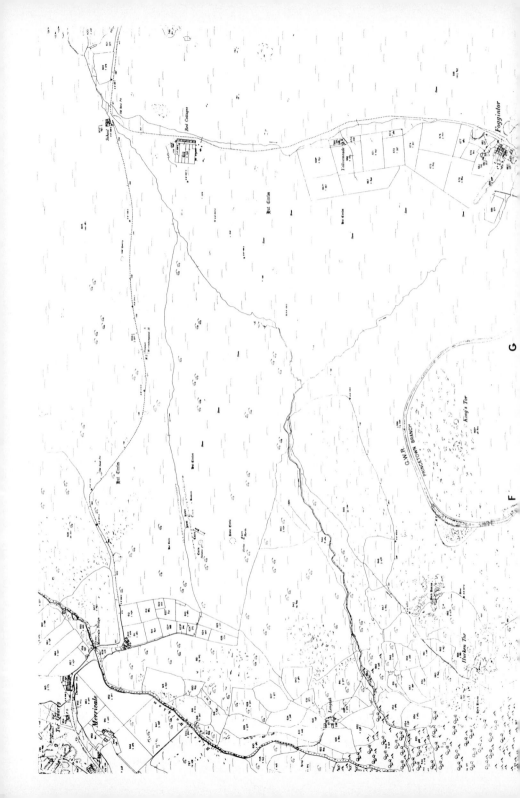

arrangement on the inclines on the other side of the moor, for the purpose of hauling trains up from Chagford to the high ground near Newhouse, in which vicinity there was to have been a tunnel, with another one near Nun's Cross. Across the Forest of Dartmoor itself locomotives were to have supplied the motive power. To provide water for the water wheels, dams were to have been constructed across the Blackbrook valley to the east of Princetown, and another across the valley of the Cowsie, a stream that falls into the West Dart just above Two Bridges, and yet a third about three miles north of Postbridge in the East Dart valley.

Needless to say, this railway never came to be, although the P. & D.R. declared interest in it as a potential source of full railway connection with the rest of the country. Opposition was soon to come from the more economic and sensible route from Plymouth to Exeter, around the coast and south of Dartmoor. This alternative was of course, the South Devon Railway route and plans for it had already been deposited during November 1843. The P. & D.R. declared itself 'neutral' towards it which meant that it neither opposed nor seconded it. However, by April 18th the South Devon Railway Bill was in hand and its construction made no provision for the P. & D.R. to raise capital in order to cope with traffic from the new line, nor was there a station, or exchange sidings proposed. The P. & D.R. was now definitely opposed to the proposal, but to no avail and consequently its future became more and more dependent on the larger companies then reaching Plymouth. The broad gauge S.D.R. reached Plymouth (Laira Green) in 1848 and Millbay the following year after the construction of Mutley Tunnel was completed.

It was not until 21st November, 1850 that fresh prosperity finally returned to Princetown in the shape of a convict prison. It was by then converted into a civil convict establishment and reopened on that date. During this time, in fact in 1847, the South Devon Railway Co. had purchased the section of the line between Plympton and Marsh Mills from the Plymouth & Dartmoor Co. in order to further the progress of their line to Plymouth. On 5th July, 1852, an agreement was reached between the South Devon & Tavistock Co. and Lord Morley for a line to be built to Lee Moor clayworks, so forming part of that company's scheme for a line to Tavistock. The Company's prospectus provided, inter alia, that the line be so arranged that if found desirable, it may be formed to Government establishments at Princetown, or the existing railway modified for that purpose.[1] The suggestion was brought before the Tavistock Co. in 1857 and was received favourably. It was also decided due to more pressing commitments nothing could be done at that point in time.

Following the decision in 1857 by the Tavistock Company to do nothing, nothing was in fact done, not at least for the next seventeen years. On 28th November, 1874 yet another set of plans were deposited with the Clerk of the Peace for Devon, Mr H. Ford at Exeter, this time by a company calling itself the South Devon & Princetown Railway Co. This company proposed not one, but two railways to serve Princetown. Railway No. 1 was to commence on the South Devon & Tavistock Railway line outside Yelverton tunnel at a point 12 chains from m.p. 11.

[1] G.H. Anthony — *The Tavistock, Launceston & Princetown Railways.*

It was to run as far as Burrator in the recognised manner, but from there on was routed towards Sheeps Tor around the south and east side of what was later to become Burrator Reservoir and thence southeast of Leather Tor, east of Sharpitor and lastly running into Princetown passing en route between Leeden Tor to the north and Black and Cramber Tors to the south. The termination of railway No. 1, 7m. 4f. and 9ch. in length, was at a point 3ch. north of the Princetown to Plymouth road and 20ch. in a westerly direction from the southwest corner of the Duchy Hotel. Railway No. 2 was to run from a point 20ch. west of Princetown (7m. 2f. and 9ch. from Yelverton) and terminate outside the boundary wall of the convict prison, i.e. along the base of that wall in a westerly direction from the south gate or entrance. Again the plans did not materialise and these railways subsequently did not appear on the map.

In fact, it was to be only two years later in 1877 when the Great Western Railway was to propose a seven mile long line between Princetown and the Plymouth & Tavistock Railway, of which they were now in possession. The GWR later withdrew this scheme in favour of yet another, made by the Plymouth & Dartmoor Co., proposing that they should sell their line from Princetown to Yelverton Junction, forming in the process a new company to be named the 'Princetown Railway Company'. Plans were duly deposited on 30th November, 1877 for a line 10 miles 2 furlongs and 3 chains long from a junction at Yelverton, just south of the tunnel under Roborough Down, to Princetown over much of the old P. & D.R. circuitous route to Princetown. The Bill dated 16th July, 1878, became law on 13th August, 1878 and contained an agreement dated 18th January, 1883 between the P. & D.R. Co and the GWR that the latter company should, not only work the line, but have controlling interest in it. This was to be the railway to Princetown known to the many generations likely to read this account. It opened amid scant celebrations on 11th August, 1883.

EXTRACTS FROM MINUTE BOOKS OF THE PRINCETOWN RAILWAY COMPANY

At a meeting of the Board of Directors held at the Great Western Railway Station, Paddington

Thursday 7th August, 1879

Present: Sir Daniel Gooch Bart MP, Sir C Alexander Wood, Sir Massey Lopes Bart MP, Henry Brown Esq., J N Batten Esq.,

Resolved that Sir Daniel Gooch Bart MP be appointed Chairman of the Board for the current year

Resolved that Mr A L Jenkins be appointed Secretary to the Company at a salary of £50 per annum which is to cover any expense of clerks' assistance for office work.

Mr Nelson explained the position of negotiation with the prison authorities with regard to the aid to be given by convict labour for part-construction of the Railway.

Resolved that Mr W Owen be the Companys' Engineer and that he be instructed to take the necessary measures for the preparation of the land plans.

Meeting of Board of Directors 12th November, 1879

Mr Nelson, the solicitor, explained that the Convict Prison authorities had hitherto objected to find any implements or materials in the aid to be given by them in the construction of the line and would supply convict labour only which, in consequence of the light nature of the works at the prison end of the line could not easily be arranged for to the agreed value of £5000.

Mr Owen was instructed to prepare a written specification of the description of assistance required from the Convict Department.

Meeting of Board of Directors 22nd April, 1880

Resolved that Sir Daniel Gooch Bart MP be and hereby is appointed Chairman of the Board for the ensuing year.

Submitted correspondence with the Convict Prisons Department and the Home Office by which it appeared from the letter dated 29th January, 1880, signed Godfrey Lushington, that Mr Cross the Secretary of State declined to contribute more than convict labour towards the proposed Railway.

Read report dated 18th April from Mr Owen the Engineer to the effect that no contractor would consider the aid of convicts of any value if he had to supply them with implements and materials. It appearing that some expense might be saved if the line were to stop short at the roadway leaving Princetown, being at the limits of the authorized line, instead of being extended as proposed close to the Prison.

Resolved that the Engineer be instructed to prepare plans of specification accordingly with a view to tenders for the works being advertised for — the work to achieve a temporary station at the point named, leaving any extension for subsequent arrangement with the Prison authorities.

Meeting of Board of Directors 24th June, 1880

Opened 17 tenders for the construction of the line

No.	Name		Amount	
1.	Joseph Phillips		£24,900	
2.	James Taylor		24,815	
3.	John Pethick		42,639	
4.	Wm Thos Mousley	2	21,800	
5.	Wm Moss		28,119 10s 7d	(£28,119.53p)
6.	Benym Winter & Co		27,260	
7.	John Mackay	3	22,190 8s 6d	(£22,190.42½p)
8.	N B Fogg & Co		37,717 4s 7d	(£37.717.23p)
9.	Robt T Relf		24,500	
10.	Rob Ward & Co		31,341	
11.	Lang & Sons		24,850 11s 5d	(£24,850.57½p)
12.	Wm Lean	4	23,332 14s 6d	(£23,332.72½p)
13.	Hubbard & Co		31,500	
14.	Mark Moses		32,197 11s 0d	(£32,197.55p)
15.	Hill Brothers	1	18,589 10s 4d	(£18,589.52p)
16.	Robt Rendell Facey		55,000	
17.	Henry Stevens		37,127 12s 2d	(£37,127.61p)

The tenders were handed to the Engineer to make enquiries and report with regard to the four lowest.

Resolved . . . . . also that the Great Western Railway Company be invited to state whether, without making a formal sale, they could arrange and on what terms to supply the permanent way materials which may eventually be required for making the line.

Sir Massey Lopes called attention to his agreement with the Promoters dated 23rd July, 1878 under which he was to provide a local subscription for £7000 towards the Company's capital and stated that having handed in a subscription contract for shares representing rather more than that amount he had fulfilled his engagement and was entitled to a release.

Mr Nelson was requested to look into the matter and report.

Meeting of Board of Directors 8th July, 1880

In reference to minute 2 of the last Board.

Read report dated 6th July from Mr Owen the Engineer on some of the tenders then opened for the construction of the line and the Secretary was authorised to inform Mr W T Mousley of 1 Westminster Chambers that provided it be decided to go on with the works his tender is accepted at £21,800.

Read letter dated 2nd July from the Honble A F D Liddell intimating that Sir W Vernon Harcourt had nothing to add to the Home Office letter of 29th January last and thought it unnecessary for the Directors to attend on a Deputation.

The Board feeling strongly that they are entitled to substantial Government aid in one form or other to the value of £5000 in conformity with the inducements held out to the Promoters when they were obtaining their Act, the Chairman and Sir Massey Lopes were requested to endeavour to bring the matter under the personal cognisance of the Home Secretary.

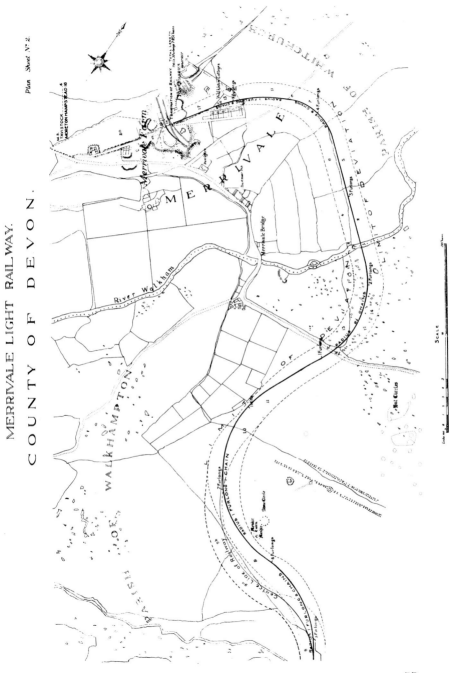

MERRIVALE LIGHT RAILWAY.

COUNTY OF DEVON.

Plan Sheet No. 2

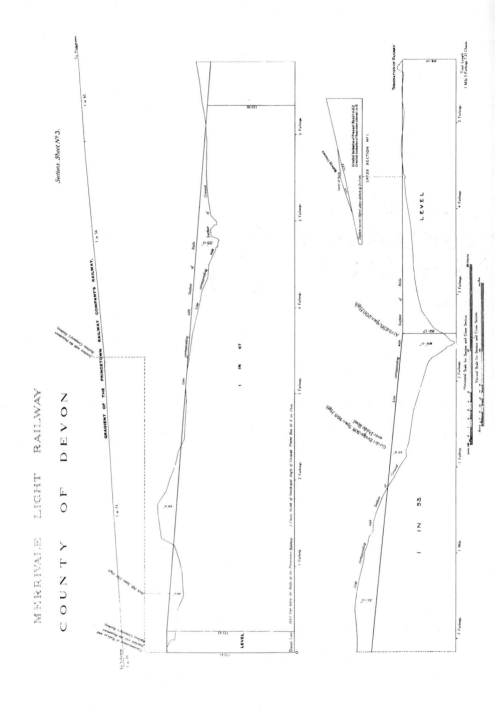

In the freezing winter of 1947, the worst snows struck the West Country since the 1891 blizzard. These scenes, near King Tor, show 0-6-0PT No 1990 complete with snow plough and three brake vans of naval personnel from H.M. Dockyard, Devonport, a) digging out the train and b) posing for the local newspaper.

Western Morning News

MORNING NEWS, SATURDAY, FEBRUARY 1, 1947.

SNOW-PLOUGH ATTEMPTS TO RAISE THE "SIEGE" OF PRINCETOWN

A snow-plough set out yesterday afternoon from Yelverton in an attempt to clear the line to Princetown and relieve the storm-beleaguered inhabitants of the Dartmoor village, who have been isolated since Wednesday. This picture was taken by a "Western Morning News" photographer in the failing light at Dousland as helpers cleared the deep drifts blocking the level crossing gates.

A snow scene at Dousland Crossing featured in the *Western Morning News* of 1 February 1947.

90

PART 4
Nationalisation to Closure and Lifting 1948–1956
History to Date

A change of ownership occurred again in 1948 when the nation's railways became nationalised on the 1st January of that year. The Princetown branch became part of British Railways (Western Region), but it was to be not for long however. The 'writing was on the wall' as early as 1954, when the first utterings of possible closure were heard. During 1955 the staff on the line were officially informed of the pending closure. The public were told the line would cease to function after December 31st that year. All through the latter months of 1955 and the early months of 1956, the passenger traffic was augmented by people making the journey as an act of sentimentality. It was as though the line were trying to reverse the very decision of closure. People came from near and far to ride the line, sometimes whole families made the pilgrimage, and for many it was to be their first as well as their last chance to do so.

It was not until Saturday March 3rd, 1956 that the line actually closed, precluded by many weeks of protestations by various bodies of objectors. The Ministry of Transport were deaf to all the complaints of inadequate roads in the area, the same often blocked by snow and Princetown being isolated as a result. On the final day Yelverton was besieged with cars as hundreds of people made the journey for the last time, attending the last obsequies of the line. Early in the following year, the demolition contractor was at work. The destruction lasted during most of 1957 and by the end of the year all the track, signalling and level crossing equipment had gone. For quite a time odd things remained; the station nameboard at Princetown, where the station was almost intact; the wire fencing marking the boundaries of the line's tortuous route; most of the platform at Ingra Tor, — even the famous 'snake notice', by then very faint indeed! Although King Tor and Burrator disappeared, the stone base of the platform and the iron 'kissing gate' of the latter, leading down to the dam remained and does so even today. The first sale of land from the defunct railway was reported in the *Western Independent* of 16th February, 1958. British Railways had just completed the sale of 11.78 acres of land around and including Lowery Crossing for only £65. It was sold to Plymouth Corporation for its adjoined land already held by them in the Burrator catchment area. Questions were asked locally at the time why the land was sold so cheaply. British Railways replied that the land consisted of fencing, an unoccupied cottage and other fitments requiring removal. They added that by selling it thus, avoided the expense to them of the

Two grey and sad scenes at Princetown station just after closure. They feature, top, the engine shed and water crane with the last piles of loco ash; lower, the goods shed, coaling stage and turntable with the passenger platform just in view, far left.   *W.E. Stevens*

Top, No. 4542 awaits departure from Princetown with a train for Yelverton on 13th August 1955.   *W.E. Stevens*

Lower, Driver Grough struggles to fill the bunker of No. 4568 at the coaling stage during a snowy day on 20th February 1956. Closure is only weeks away.

R.C. Sambourne

Two 45XX tanks, Nos. 4568 and 4583 head a train for Princetown across the downs at Yennadon, on the last day of working. The crews were Enginemen W. Gough and F. Coles; Firemen C. Stephens and R. Hext; Guard K. Gay.

Author's Collection

A small cluster of travellers are grouped around the station building at Dousland as they await the arrival of the train from Princetown. It's the 3rd March 1956, the last day of operation.

B. Kohring

(c)

(d)

(e)

(f)

99

(g)

(h)

(i)

(j)

Llynvi & Ogmore Railway 0-6-0T No. 1
As G.W.R. No. 919
Built by Sharp, Stewart & Co., 1865

		a.m.	*a.m.*	*p.m.*	*p.m.*
Plymouth	dep.	8.15	11.20	2.20	5.55
			p.m.		
Horrabridge	arr.	8.57	12.4	3.5	6.37
Horrabridge	dep.	9.5	12.8	3.16	6.42
Dousland	dep.	9.16	12.19	3.27	6.53
Princetown	arr.	9.42	12.45	3.53	7.20
Princetown	dep.	8.12	10.52	2.17	5.42
Dousland	dep.	8.36	11.16	2.41	6.6
Horrabridge	arr.	8.45	11.25	2.50	6.15
Horrabridge	dep.	8.58	11.31	3.8	6.25
			p.m.		
Plymouth	arr.	9.35	12.15	3.51	7.10

The first locomotive and the first timetable on the branch, circa 1883.

G. W. R.

Dousland

Plymouth, Princetown, Tavistock, and Launceston.

DOWN TRAINS.

	WEEK DAYS.	SUNDAYS.
PLYMOUTH { MILLBAY dep.		
NORTH RD.		
MUTLEY		
MARSH MILLS		
BICKLEIGH		
YELVERTON		
PRINCETOWN arr.		
YELVERTON dep.		
DOUSLAND		
HORRABRIDGE		
TAVISTOCK		
MARYTAVY		
LIDFORD		
CORYTON		
LIFTON		
LAUNCESTON arr.		

UP TRAINS.

	WEEK DAYS.	SUNDAYS.
LAUNCESTON dep.		
LIFTON		
CORYTON		
LIDFORD		
MARYTAVY		
TAVISTOCK		
HORRABRIDGE		
PRINCETOWN dep.		
DOUSLAND		
YELVERTON		
YELVERTON		
BICKLEIGH		
MARSH MILLS		
PLYMOUTH { MUTLEY arr.		
{ MILLBAY		

Jan. – Apl. 1896.

Plymouth, Princetown, Tavistock and Launceston.

	WEEK DAYS.	SUNDAYS.
PLYMTH { MILLB'Y dep.		
{ Mutley		
MARSH MILLS		
BICKLEIGH		
YELVERTON		
YELVERTON dep.		
DOUSLAND		
PRINCETOWN arr.		
HORRABRIDGE		
TAVISTOCK		
MARYTAVY		
LIDFORD		
CORYTON		
LIFTON		
LAUNCESTON arr.		

	WEEK DAYS.	SUNDAYS.
LAUNCEST'N dep.		
LIFTON		
CORYTON		
LIDFORD		
MART'VY		
TAVISTO.		
HORRABRIDGE		
PRINCET'N dep.		
DOUSLAN.		
YELVER. on arr.		
YELVERTON dep.		
BICKLEIGH		
MARSH MILLS		
PLY. { Mutley arr.		
MTH { N.Rd.		
{ Millby		

Jan. – Apl. 1905.

(7-8) PLYMOUTH, PRINCETOWN, TAVISTOCK, LAUNCESTON. G.W.R.

	WEEK DAYS																				SUNDAYS			
	AM	AM	AM	AM	AM	AM	PM	PM	PM	PM	PM	PM	PM	PM	AM	PM	PM	PM	AM	PM	PM	PM
PLYMOUTH ....d.	6 20	7 35	8 30	1040	1145	2 0	2 55	5 10	6 10	8 20	9 50	1113	1030	2 0	5 45	8 15
North Road	6 25	7 40	8 35	1045	1150	2 5	3 0	5 15	6 15	8 25	9 54	1118	1035	2 5	5 50	8 20
Mutley	6 27	7 42	8 38	1048	1152	2 8	3 3	5 17	6 18	28	9 56	1120	1038	2 8	5 52	8 22
Marsh Mills	6 33	7 48	8 50	1054	1158	2 15	3 10	5 23	6 24	8 31	10 2	1125	1044	2 14	5 58	8 28
Plym Bridge Platform					12 2	2 19	3 15	5 27				1049	2 19	6 3	8 32
Bickleigh	6 44	8 0	9 0	11 9	1212	2 31	3 30	5 35	6 34	8 47	1012	1136	1057	2 27	5 11	8 40
Shaugh Bridge Platfm.		8 5			1216	2 35	3 35	5 39	6 37	8 50		11 2	2 32	6 16	8 45
Yelverton	6 56	8 15	9 11	1122	1226	2 44	3 45	5 49	6 47	8 59	1023	1147	1112	2 42	6 24	8 55
Yelverton ....d.		8 43		1130		2 50	4 55	6 55		9 85				
Dousland		8 55		1135		2 56	5 5	7 1		9811		M	M	M	M	M
Princetown ....a.		9 28		12 3		3 26	5 28	7 28		9838				
Horrabridge	7 2	8 22	9 17	1128	1233	2 50	3 51	5 55	6 54	9 4	1029	1153	1118	2 48		9 0
Whitchurch Down Plat.	7 9	8 29	9 24	1136	1240	2 57	3 59	6 3	7 1	9 11	1037	12 0	1125	2 55		9 7
Tavistock	7 12	8 34	9 27	1140	1243	3 0	4 9	6 6	7 9	9 14	1040	12 3	1128	3 0		9 10
Marytavy & Blackdown		8 43			1257		4 18		7 18
Lydford		8 52			1 6		4 27		7 27
Coryton		9 3			1 15		4 36		7 36
Lifton		9 11			1 23		4 44		7 44
LAUNCESTON ....a.		9 21			1 33		4 54		7 54

s Runs Sats. only.

(9-10) LAUNCESTON, TAVISTOCK, PRINCETOWN, PLYMOUTH. G.W.R.

	WEEK DAYS																	SUNDAYS			
	AM	AM	AM	AM	PM	PM	PM	PM	PM	PM	PM	PM	nht.	AM	PM	PM	PM	PM
LAUNCESTON ....d.	7 20		9 52	2 15	6 25					
Lifton	7 31		10 3	2 24	6 34			M	M	M	M
Coryton	7 40		1011	2 32	6 41
Lydford	7 54		1024	2 46	7 2
Marytavy & Blackdown	8 2		1032	2 54	7 2
Tavistock	7 32	8 10	9 33	1040	1250	3 24	6 28	7 13	9 45	1050	1210	1140	4 35	9 20
Whitchurch Down Plat.	7 35	8 13	9 36	1043	1253	3 5	4 33	6 31	7 16	9 48	1213	1143	4 38	9 23
Horrabridge	7 42	8 24	9 44	1052		3 14	4 41	6 40	7 25	9 56	11 0	1222	1152	4 46	9 32
Princetown ....d.		7 38		1015	S 1225	4 5	6 5	8s20		M
Dousland		8 6		1043	S 1253	4 35	6 33	8s48
Yelverton ....a.		8 11		1048	S 1258	4 40	6 38	8s53
Yelverton	7 48	8 31	9 49	1059	1 7	3 19	4 48	6 46	7 32	10 2	11 6	1228	1159	6 35	9 39
Shaugh Bridge Platfm.	7 54	8 37	9 55		1 13	3 25	4 54	6 52	7 38	10 8		12 5	4 59	42	9 45
Bickleigh	8 0	8 41	9 58	11 8	1 17	3 29	4 58	6 55	7 46	1013	1116	1236	1203	3 6	46	9 50
Plym Bridge Platform			10 5		1 24		5 5	7 3	7 54	1020		1217	5 10	6	54	9 57
Marsh Mills	8 10	8 49	10 8	1116	1 27	3 37	5 9	7 6	7 57	rm.	1023	1126	1245	1203	5 10	57	10 0
Mutley	8 15	8 54	1013	1122	1 32	3 43	5 14	7 11	8 3	1028	1131	1252	1227	5 19	7	2 10 6
North Road	8 18	8 57	1015	1125	1 34	3 46	5 17	7 14	8 8	1031	1133	1254	1230	5 22	7	1010
PLYMOUTH	8 25	9 4	1022	1134	1 42	3 53	5 26	7 20	8 13	1040	1139	1359	1255	5 28	7 12	1016

S Sats. only.   M Rail Motor.

Passenger Timetable — Jan 1925.

EXCURSIONS!!

A NUMBER OF ATTRACTIVE TRIPS HAVE BEEN ARRANGED.
DAY AND HALF-DAY EXCURSIONS TO ALL PARTS.
Watch Special Announcements!

PLYMOUTH, PRINCETOWN, TAVISTOCK AND LAUNCESTON.
(A Special Service of Fast Trains will run on this Branch on Bank Holidays—see handbills.)

			WEEK-DAYS.															SUNDAYS.			
		M			M	M					M					M		M				
		a.m.	a.m.	a.m.	a.m.	a.m.	p.m.	p.m.		p.m.	p.m.	p.m.	p.m.	p.m.		p.m.	p.m.		p.m.		a.m.	p.m. p.m. p.m. p.m. p.m. p.m.
Plymouth { Millbay .. *dep.*		6 20	7 0	7 33	8 25	10 40	12 10	12 14		2 8	3 5	4 30	5 25	6 10		7 14	9 5		11 10		10 35 2 5 4 20 7 20 8 25
{ North Road		6 25	7 4	7 50	8 30	10 44	12 14	12 19		2 12	3 10	4 34	5 29	6 16		7 17	9 10		11 14		10 40 2 10 4 35 7 25 8 31
{ Mutley		6 27	7 6	7 52	8 32	10 46	12 16	12 21		2 14	3 12	4 36	5 31	6 18		7 19	9 12		11 16		10 42 2 12 4 38 7 27 8 33
Marsh Mills		6 33	7 12	7 58	8 40	10 52	12 22	12 27		2 20	3 18	4 43	5 37	6 24		7 25	9 18		11 22		10 48 2 18 4 45 7 33 8 39
Plym Bridge Platform						10 56	12 25	1 0		2 24	3 21		5 40			7 28					10 51 2 21 .. .. 8 42
Bickleigh		6 42	7 20	8 6	8 48	11 3	12 32	1 12		2 30	3 30	4 57	5 47	6 32		7 39	9 28		11 30		10 58 2 28 4 55 7 43 8 50
Shaugh Bridge Platform				8 10	8 52	11 7	12 36	1 15		2 34	3 34	5 0	5 51	6 36		7 42	9 32		11 34		11 2 2 32 4 58 7 46 8 53
Clearbrook Halt				8 15	8 57	11 12	12 41	1 21		2 39	3 38	5 6	5 56	6 41		7 47	9 37		11 39		11 8 2 38 5 4 7 52 8 59
Yelverton .. *arr*		6 51	7 29	8 19	9 0	11 15	12 45	1 25		2 43	3 42	5 9	5 59	6 44		7 51	9 40		11 42		11 12 2 42 5 7 7 55 9 2
Yelverton .. *dep.*				8 36		11 23				2 50	IV51	5W12		6 55			9W17				
Dousland				8 41		11 29				2 56	IV57	5W18		7 1			9W25				
Burrator Halt				8 54		11 35				3 2	3V	5W24		7 7							
Ingra Tor Halt ..				9 9		11 47				3 14	3V15	5W26		7 19							
King Tor Halt ..				9 22		11 58				3 25	3V26	5W47		7 30			10W11				
Princetown .. *arr.*				9 31		12 5				3 32	3V32	5W57		7 36			10W20				
Yelverton .. *dep.*		6 53	7 32	8 22	9 4	11 19	12 48	1 26		2 45	3 45		6 2	6 48		7 54	9 43		11 43		11 15 2 45 .. .. 9 5
Horrabridge		6 57	7 36	8 26	9 8	11 25	12 55	1 30		2 49	3 50		6 6	6 54		7 58	9 47		11 47		11 19 2 49 .. .. 9 9
Whitchurch Down Platform ..		7	2	7 41	8 31	9 13	11 28	1 0	1 34		2 53	3 54		6 11	6 59		8 3	9 52		11 52		11 26 2 56 .. .. 9 16
Tavistock *		7	5	7 44	8X45	9 16	11 31	1 8	1 39		3 0	4 0		6 14	7 9		8 6	9 55		11 55		11 30 3 0 .. .. 9 20
Marytavy and Blackdown				8 54		1 17				4 6			7 16			10 15					
Lydford §				9 3		1 25				4 14			7 23			10 23					
Coryton				9 13		1 34				4 24			7 32			10 30					
Lifton				9 23		1 42				4 30			7 39			10 40					
Launceston .. *arr.*				9 31		1 52				4 38			7 47			10 50					

M One class only. **V** Wednesdays and Saturdays excepted. **W** Wednesdays and Saturdays only. **X** Tavistock arrive 8.34 a.m. * Five minutes later on Tuesdays and Saturdays only. † North Road arrive 7.36 a.m. ‡ Tavistock arrive 7.2 p.m. ¶ One mile to Southern Railway Station. § Adjoins Southern Railway Station.

EVENING EXCURSIONS.

Evening Excursion Bookings, at specially reduced rates, are given between certain Stations and Shopping Centres, Seaside Resorts, etc., by specified services.
Ask at Stations for handbill of these facilities.

LAUNCESTON, TAVISTOCK, PRINCETOWN AND PLYMOUTH.
(A Special Service of Fast Trains will run on this Branch on August Bank Holiday—see handbills).

		WEEK-DAYS.												SUNDAYS.					
		a.m.	a.m.	a.m.	a.m.	p.m.	p.m.		p.m.	p.m.	p.m.	p.m.	p.m.	night	a.m.	p.m.	p.m.	p.m.	p.m. p.m.
Launceston .. *dep.*		7 22		10 17			2 20			6 25		9 25							
Lifton		7 31		10 26			2 29			6 34		9 34							
Coryton		7 38		10 33			2 36			6 41		9 41							
Lydford§		7 50		10 45			2 48			6 53		9 54							
Marytavy and Blackdown		7 57		10 52			2 55		M		7 0	M	10 7						
Tavistock ¶		7 15	8 5	8 47	9 30	11 0	12 45	1 48	3 6	6 30	7 11	8 30	10 7	10 10	12 0	11 50	3 15		9 25
Whitchurch Down Platform ..		7 18	8 8	8 50	9 33	11 3	12 48	1 51	3 6	6 33	7 14	8 33		10 13	12 3	11 52	3 18		9 28
Horrabridge		7 25	8 15	8 57	9 40	11 10	12 55	1 58	3 13	6 40	7 22	8 40		10 20	12 10	12 1	3 26		9 36
Yelverton .. *arr*		7 29	8 19	9 1	9 45	11 14	1 0		3 17	6 45	7 26	8 44		10 24	12 14	12 6	3 30		9 40
Princetown .. *dep.*		7 40		10 30	12T14		4 0		6 0		8W 0							
King Tor Halt ..		7 45		10 39	12T20		4 5		6 5		8W 5							
Ingra Tor Halt ..		7 54		10 44	12T30		4 14		6 14		8W14							
Burrator Halt ..		8 6		10 45	12T42		4 26		6 26		8W26							
Dousland		8 10		11 3	12T49		4 32		6 32		8W32							
Yelverton .. *arr.*		8 16		11 8	12T55		4 38		6 38		8W38							
Yelverton .. *dep.*		7 30	8 20	9 2	9 46	11 16	1 2	2 3	3 18	4 46	5 35	6 48	7 28	8 45	10 25	12 15	12 8	3 31	6 25 8 9 10 9 41
Clearbrook Halt ..		7 33	8 23		9 49	11 19	1 4		3 21	4 49	5 38	6 51	7 34	8 51	10 28		12 11	3 34	6 28 8 3 9 7 19 48
Shaugh Bridge Platform ..		7 36	8 26		9 52	11 22	1 8		3 24	4 52	5 41	6 57	7 38	8 51	10 31		12 15	3 38	6 28 3 7 9 17 9 48
Bickleigh ..		7 39	8 30	9 10	9 55	11 26	1 12	2 10	3 28	4 55	5 48	6 57	7 38	8 55	10 35	12 23	12 18	3 41	6 35 8 10 9 20 9 51
Plym Bridge Platform ..		7 47	8 39		10 4	11 34	1 18			5 0	5 53			9 0			12 23		9 56
Marsh Mills .. *arr.*		7 52	8 44		10 10	11 39	1 28	2 22	3 33	5 4	5 57	7 7	7 51	9 10	10 43		12 27	3 55	6 50 8 23 9 33 10 5
Plymouth { Mutley ..		7 58	8 49		10 15	11 46	1 34	2 28	3 41	5 10	6 3	7 12	7 51	9 15	10 49		12 32	3 56	6 56 8 18 9 28 10 0
{ North Road ..		8 0	8 52		10 20	11 47	1 35		3 42	5 15	6 4	7 17	7 59	9 20	10 51	12 37		4 2	6 58 8 20 9 40 10 12
{ Millbay .. *arr.*														10 57		12 39	4 4	2 6 8 38 9 40 10 12

M One class only. **T** Tuesdays, Thursdays and Saturdays only. **W** Wednesdays and Saturdays only. **¶** One mile to Southern Railway Station. § Adjoins Southern Railway Station.

Passenger Timetable. Period 6th Jul. 1936 — 27th Sep. 1936.

97

How can a town 1300 ft above sea level flood? This Devon Motor Transport 'A.E.C.' is left stranded in the water outside 'The Prince of Wales' Inn, Princetown on a very wet day in 1925.   *H. Pitts Collection*

A Cornish Motor Transport 'Thornycroft', No 2081 poses with its crew and (another)? on a drier day on the same location and year. The name board reads "Princetown-Merrivale-Tavistock" a far cry from its original stable for this London General Omnibus.   *H. Pitts Collection*

Saturdays and Sundays only.

Tavistock (Bedford Square) *dep*	...	1230	...	...	7 15	...	...	...
Taviton ... ... ,,	...	1235	...	...	7 20	...	...	...
Moorshop ... ... ,,	...	1240	...	...	7 25	...	...	...
Merrivale ... ... ,,	...	1253	...	...	7 38	...	...	...
Foggintor ... ... ,,	...	1 2	...	...	7 47	...	...	...
Rendlestone ... ... ,,	...	1 7	...	...	7 52	...	...	...
Princetown (Square) ... *arr*	...	1 12	...	...	7 57	...	...	...

Princetown (Square) ... *dep*	...	1 15	...	...	8 0	...	...	...
Rendlestone ... ... ,,	...	1 20	...	...	8 5	...	...	...
Foggintor ... ... ,,	...	1 25	...	...	8 10	...	...	...
Merrivale ... ... ,,	...	1 31	...	...	8 16	...	...	...
Moorshop ... ... ,,	...	1 43	...	...	8 28	...	...	...
Taviton ... ... ,,	...	1 47	...	...	8 32	...	...	...
Tavistock (Bedford Square) *arr*	...	1 52	...	...	8 37	...	...	...

𝔅𝔯𝔦𝔱𝔞𝔦𝔫 𝔄𝔴𝔞𝔦𝔱𝔰 !

—DAYS WHEN THE EASE AND COMFORT OF ROAD TRAVEL WILL ENABLE US TO SEE THE BEAUTIES OF OUR OWN COUNTRY.

Western National Omnibus Timetable for route 113. Period from Jul. 1945.

113 | H 665 | TAVISTOCK—PRINCETOWN—YELVERTON. | 113
(Showing connections at Yelverton to and from Plymouth.)

	Tuesdays and Fridays.			Saturdays.					Thro' Fares from Tavistock	
									Single	Return
Tavistock (Bedford Square)... dep	9 10	3 0	...	9 10	1 20	9 30	...	...	4d	—
Taviton ... ,,	9 15	3 5	...	9 15	1 25	9 35	...	...	4d	—
Moorshop ... ,,	9 20	3 10	...	9 20	1 30	9 40	...	...	6d	—
Merrivale (Dartmoor Inn) ,,	9 33	3 23	...	9 33	1 43	9 53	...	...	11d	—
Foggintor (School) ,,	9 42	3 32	...	9 42	1 52	10 2	...	...	1/1	—
Rendlestone ... ,,	9 47	3 37	...	9 47	1 57	10 7	...	...	1/4	—
Princetown (Square) ... ,,	9 52	3 42	...	9 52	2 2	10 12	...	...	1/7	2/8
Peek Hill ... ,,			...	10 2	2 12	10 22	...	...	2/-	—
Dousland (Manor Hotel) ,,	...	...		10 13	2 23	10 33	...	...	2/2	—
Yelverton (Roundabout) arr	...	...		10 17	2 27	10 37	...	...	2/4	—
Ser. 83 Yelverton (Roundab't) dep	...	...	...	10 19	2 51	10 54	...	...	—	—
Ser. 83 **Plymouth** (Bus Stn.) ... arr	...	...	...	10 55	3 27	11 30	...	...	—	—
Ser. 83 **Plymouth** (Bus Stn.) ... dep	...	...	...	9 30	1 30	10 0	...	...	—	—
Ser. 83 Yelverton (Roundab't) arr	...	...	...	10 6	2 6	10 36	...	...	—	—

	Tuesdays and Fridays.			Saturdays.					Thro' Fares from Yelverton	
									Single	Return
Yelverton (Roundabout) ... dep	...	...	...	10 35	2 35	10 40	...	...	3d	—
Dousland (Manor Hotel) ,,	...	...	...	10 39	2 39	10 44	...	...	7d	—
Peek Hill ... ,,			...	10 50	2 50	10 55	...	...	1/2	2/-
Princetown (Square) ... ,,	9 55	3 45	...	11 0	3 0	11 5	...	...	1/5	—
Rendlestone ... ,,	10 0	3 50	...	11 5	3 5	11 10	...	...	1/7	—
Foggintor (School) ... ,,	10 5	3 55	...	11 10	3 10	11 15	...	...	1/8	—
Merrivale (Dartmoor Inn) ,,	10 11	4 1	...	11 16	3 16	11 21	...	...	2/1	—
Moorshop ... ,,	10 23	4 13	...	11 28	3 28	11 33	...	...	2/2	—
Taviton ... ,,	10 27	4 17	...	11 32	3 32	11 37	...	...	2/4	—
Tavistock (Bedford Square) arr	10 32	4 22	...	11 37	3 37	11 42	...	...		

Coaches for Private Parties are available for hire

Ask at any of the Company's local offices for quotations & helpful suggestions without obligation

53

17/1/54

Western National Omnibus Timetable for route 113. Period from 17th Jan. 1954.

Western National Service 113 prior to the closure of the Princetown Branch.
Timetable from 11th September, 1955 (no service on Mondays, Wednesdays, Thursdays and Winter Sundays).

	Tuesdays and Fridays		Saturdays			Summer Sundays	
	am	pm	am	pm	pm	pm	pm
Tavistock (Bedford Square)	9 0	2 45	8 50	1 20	8 20	1*45	7*45
Princetown (Square)	9 32	3 17	9 22	1 52	8 52	2*17	8*17
Dousland (Manor Hotel)	....	....	9 40	2 10	9 10	....	....
Yelverton (Roundabout)	....	....	9 44	2 14	9 14	....	....
			am	pm	pm		
Bus to Plymouth departs	....	....	9 51	2 19	9 19	....	....
			am	pm	pm		
Bus from Plymouth arrives	....	....	9 36	2 6	9 6	....	....
	am	pm	am	pm	pm	pm	pm
Yelverton (Roundabout)	....	....	9 47	2 17	9 17	....	....
Dousland (Manor Hotel)	....	....	9 51	2 21	9 21	....	....
Princetown (Square)	9 40	3 20	10 9	2 39	9 39	2*20	8*20
Tavistock (Bedford Square)	1012	3 52	1041	3 11	1011	2*52	8*52

* - 17th June to 2nd September, 1956.

Railway Replacement Journeys operated ADDITIONALLY to those shown above.
Extra journeys, providing a service every Weekday, introduced 5th March, 1956.

	Mondays to Fridays				Saturdays			
	am	am	pm	pm	am	am	pm	pm
Tavistock (Bedford Square)	7 13	10 1	4 29	6 33	7 13	10 1	.....	6 33
Princetown (Square)	7 45	10 33	H	H	7 45	10 33	12 23	H
Dousland (Manor Hotel)	8 3	10 51	H	H	8 3	10 51	12 41	H
Yelverton (Roundabout)	8R 7	10R55	4 48	6 52	8R 7	10R55	12R45	6 52
	am	am			am	am		
Train to Plymouth departs	8 16	11 18	....	....	8 16	11 18	12 50	....
			pm	pm				pm
Train from Plymouth arrives	....	.....	4B50	6 54	....	.....	.....	6 54
	am	pm	pm	pm	am	am		pm
Yelverton (Roundabout)	8 10	11 0	4R51	7R 0	8 10	11 0	.....	7R 0
Dousland (Manor Hotel)	H	H	4 55	7 4	H	H	.....	7 4
Princetown (Square)	H	H	5 13	7 22	H	H	.....	7 22
Tavistock (Bedford Square)	8 29	11 19	5 45	7 54	8 29	11 19	.....	7 54

R - Operated to and from Yelverton (Railway Station).   B - Bus arrival at Yelverton (Roundabout).
H - Via Horrabridge.

Apart from small adjustments to the point to point timings, the above timetables applied until 20th June, 1959.

Revised Timetable introduced 22nd June, 1959 (Summer Sunday service withdrawn).

	Mondays to Fridays						Saturdays				
		FO	TFO	WO	TFO						
	am	am	am	pm	pm	pm	am	am	pm	pm	pm
Tavistock (Bus Station)	6 57	9 0	10 55	2 30	2 40	6 5	6 57	8 53	1 27	6 5	10 20
Princetown (Square)	7 31	9 34	11 29	H	3 14	6 39	7 31	9 27	2 1	6 39	H
Dousland (Manor Hotel)	7 49	....	11 47	H	....	6 57	7 49	9 45	2 19	6 57	H
Yelverton (Roundabout)	7 53	....	11 51	2 51	....	7 1	7 53	9 49	2 23	7 1	10 41
Yelverton (Railway Station)	7 55	....	.....	....	....	7 3	7 55	....	....	7 3	.....
	am		am			pm	am	am	pm	pm	
Train to Plymouth departs	8 18	....	11B54	....	....	7 26	8 18	9B49	2B23	7 26	.....
	am		noon	pm		pm	am	am	pm	pm	pm
Train from Plymouth arrives	7 44	....	12B 0	2B53	....	6 50	7 44	9B50	2B 6	6 50	10B40
		FO	TFO	WO	TFO						
	am	am	pm	pm	pm	pm	am	am	pm	pm	pm
Yelverton (Railway Station)	8 0	....	....	....	....	7 8	8 0	....	....	7 8	.....
Yelverton (Roundabout)	8 2	....	12 0	2 57	....	7 10	8 2	9 54	2 28	7 10	10 46
Dousland (Manor Hotel)	8 6	....	12 4	3 1	....	7 14	8 6	9 58	2 32	7 14	10 50
Princetown (Square)	8 24	9 40	12 22	3 19	3 19	7 32	8 24	10 16	2 50	7 32	11 8
Tavistock (Bus Station)	8 58	1014	12 56	3 53	3 53	8 6	8 58	1050	3 24	8 6	11 42

B - Bus arrival or departure at Yelverton (Roundabout).   TFO - Tuesdays and Fridays only.
H - Via Horrabridge.   FO - Fridays only.   WO - Wednesdays only.

With the following qualifications, the above timetable applied until 2nd January, 1971 :-

From 16th September, 1963, operation to and from Yelverton (Railway Station) discontinued; small adjustments
  to the timings of the affected journeys.   The Railway Station was closed on 31st December, 1962[1]
From 25th October, 1963, school journey operated from Tavistock (Drake Statue) at 4 37pm, via Tavistock (Bus
  Station) 4 40pm, returning from Princetown at 5 19pm.
From 17th June, 1967, Saturday evening late journey withdrawn.
From 3rd June, 1968, small adjustments to point to point timings.

Revised Timetable introduced 4th January, 1971 (Service truncated at Princetown on Mondays to Fridays).

Mondays to Fridays		FO	TFO	TFO	SDO		Saturdays			
	am	am	am	pm	pm	pm	am	am	pm	pm
Tavistock (Bus Station)	7 35	9 0	1135	2 45	4 25	6 5	7 35	8 55	1 30	6 5
Princetown (Square)	8 6	9 31	12 6	3 16	4 56	6 36	8 6	9 26	2 1	6 36
Dousland (Manor Hotel)	....	....	....	....	....	....	....	9 41	....	6 51
Yelverton (Roundabout)	....	....	....	....	....	....	....	9 45	....	6 55
								am		pm
Bus to Plymouth departs	....	....	....	....	....	....	....	9 49	....	7 4

		FO	TFO	TFO	SDO			am		pm
Bus from Plymouth arrives	....	....	....	....	....	....	....	9 50	....	7 6
	am	am	pm	pm	pm	pm	am	am	pm	pm
Yelverton (Roundabout)	....	....	....	....	....	....	....	9 50	....	7 6
Dousland (Manor Hotel)	....	....	....	....	....	....	....	9 54	....	7 10
Princetown (Square)	8 14	9 36	1211	3 21	7 1	6 41	8 14	10 9	2 10	7 25
Tavistock (Bus Station)	8 45	10 7	1242	3 52	7 32	7 12	8 45	1040	2 41	7 56

FO - Fridays only.   TFO - Tuesdays and Fridays only.   SDO - School Days only.

Revised Timetable introduced 6th September, 1971 (Princetown to Yelverton section abandoned).
No Public Transport facilities between Princetown and Dousland; Dousland to Yelverton continued to be served by Plymouth Joint Service 56, operated Weekdays and Sundays.

Weekdays		FSO	FO	SO	FO			FSO	FO	SO	FO
	am	am	am	pm	pm	pm		am	am	pm	pm	pm	pm
Tavistock (Bus Station)	7 35	9 0	1130	1 30	2 45	4 25	Princetown (Square)	8 14	9 36	12 6	2 10	3 21	5 1
Princetown (Square)	8 6	9 31	12 1	2 1	3 16	4 56	Tavistock (Bus Station)	8 45	10 7	1237	2 41	3 52	5 32

FSO - Fridays and Saturdays only.   FO - Fridays only.   SO - Saturdays only.

After operation on 5th May, 1973, Western National Service 113 was discontinued.   From 7th May, 1973, the service was uplifted by J.R. Striplin of Tavistock: the timetable introduced by Western National on 6th September, 1971 continues to be operated, but with small adjustments to the point to point timings.

New Plymouth Joint Service 56B introduced 8th June, 1975 (initially operated Summer Sundays only - see footnote)
First Public Transport facility to and from Burrator since the closure of the Princetown Branch.

Summer Sundays only (see footnote)									55A		
	am	am	am	pm	pm	pm	pm	pm	pm	pm	pm
Plymouth (Bus Station)	9 30	1030	1130	1230	1 30	2 30	3 30	4 30	5 10	....	6 30
Plymouth (Railway Station)	9 34	1034	1134	1234	1 34	2 34	3 34	4 34	....	....	6 34
Yelverton (Roundabout)	10 6	11 6	12 6	1 6	2 6	3 6	4 6	5 6	5 46	6 10	7 6
Dousland (Yennadon Cross)	1012	1112	1212	1 12	2 12	3 12	4 18	5 12	....	6 16	7 18
Burrator Reservoir	1023	1123	1223	1 23	2 23	3 23	4 29	5 23	....	6 27	7 29

				55A							
	am	am	pm	pm	pm	pm	pm	pm	pm	pm	pm
Burrator Reservoir	1030	1130	1226	....	1 30	2 30	3 30	4 30	5 30	6 30	7 30
Dousland (Yennadon Cross)	1041	1141	1237	....	1 41	2 41	3 41	4 41	5 41	6 41	7 41
Yelverton (Roundabout)	1053	1153	1243	1 9	1 53	2 47	3 47	4 47	5 47	6 47	7 47
Plymouth (Railway Station)	1125	1225	....	....	2 25	3 19	4 19	5 19	6 19	7 19	8 19
Plymouth (Bus Station)	1129	1229	....	1 45	2 29	3 23	4 23	5 23	6 23	7 23	8 23

Following the success of the first summer's operation (8,200 passengers carried), the service was continued on Winter Sundays, three return journeys being operated.   From 2nd May, 1976, the service was renumbered 57 and operated on Summer Weekdays (three return journeys), Summer Sundays (hourly) and Winter Sundays (three return journeys), buses carrying "Dartmoor Link" headboards ("Coastal Dartmoor Link" on Summer Sundays).

New Western National Service 82 introduced 2nd May, 1976.   Buses carry "Transmoor Link" headboards.
First Public Transport facility between Dousland and Princetown since 4th September, 1971.

Summer Saturdays and Summer Sundays only (see footnote)									
	am	am	pm	pm			am	pm	pm	pm
Plymouth (Bus Station)	9 45	1145	1 45	3 45	Moretonhampstead (Court Street)	1130	1 30	3 30	5 30
Plymouth (Railway Station)	9 49	1149	1 49	3 49	Princetown (Square)	1210	2 10	4 10	6 10
Yelverton (Roundabout)	1020	1220	2 20	4 20	Dousland (Burrator Hotel) **	1224	2 24	4 24	6 24
Dousland (Burrator Hotel) **	1026	1226	2 26	4 26	Yelverton (Roundabout)	1230	2 30	4 30	6 30
Princetown (Square)	1040	1240	2 40	4 40	Plymouth (Railway Station)	1 1	3 1	5 1	7 1
Moretonhampstead (Court Street)	1120	1 20	3 20	5 20	Plymouth (Bus Station)	1 5	3 5	5 5	7 5

** - Formerly the "Manor Hotel"
In 1977, this service was operated additionally on Wednesdays during the Summer School holidays.

No attempt is made to show the changes to Services 56B (later 57) and 82 as the timetables of both these new services have not yet "stabilized".

ENGINEERING AND OPERATING DATA.

Pages 127 to 131 are reproduced from the "Appendix to No 6 of the Service Time Table, GWR Plymouth Division — April 1939".

Pages 133 to 136 are Signal Box Diagrams of stations on the branch. They were prepared for this book by members of the Historical Signalling Society.

Page 150 carries a photograph of a Yelverton luggage label, others from the branch appear on pages 62, 90, 109 & 149.

Photographs of tickets used on the branch appear on pages 97 & 133—136.

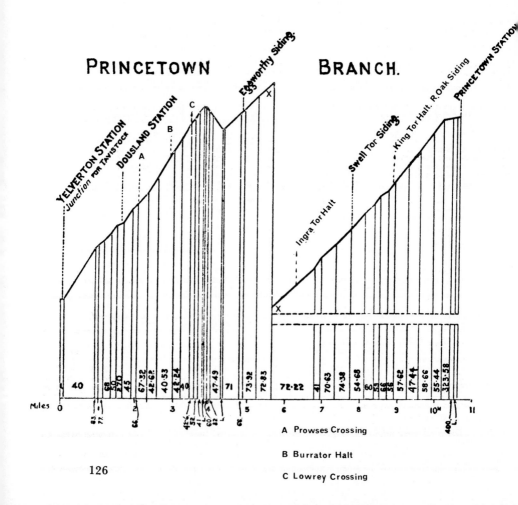

A Prowses Crossing

B Burrator Halt

C Lowrey Crossing

YELVERTON.
Shunting Princetown Trains.

1.   At Yelverton the engine must be run around the coaches of the Princetown train in the following manner :—
2.   After the passengers have left the coaches the train must be pushed towards Dousland, clear of the Siding leading to the turntable.
3.   The train must then be stopped, and after the coaches have been secured by means of the brake, the engine must be detached and run into the Turntable Siding. The coaches may then be allowed to drop down to the platform clear of the points leading to the turntable, where they must stand until the engine is attached to them.
4.   During the time the coaches are being moved in the manner described, the points must be set for the Dead End, so that the coaches cannot foul the Main line.
5.   When shunting Mixed trains and trains of unusual length, the points must be set for the Main line, instead of the Dead End, before dropping the train down to the platform, and the Guard must not drop the train down before he has asked for and received a signal from the Signalman that the points are right, and the line is clear.
6.   As the line falls rapidly towards the junction, it is of the utmost importance that the coaches should be let down to the platform very cautiously, and the Guard of the Princetown Branch trains will be held responsible for carrying out this work.

Down Shunt Siding.

The Down Refuge Siding at Yelverton is for the purpose of putting away Divided Down trains, also when a train is assisted in the rear by a second engine intended to travel with the train beyond Yelverton, for such train to be backed into the Siding, while the assistant engine is run to the head of the train either on the Up or Down line, also for Goods traffic for and from Princetown Branch.

Conveyance of Goods Traffic to Princetown.

If to facilitate the transit of important General Goods traffic to Princetown it should be necessary to put wagons off at Yelverton the following arrangements must be followed :—
The traffic must be confined to the Tavistock Goods ex Laira, to go forward by the first available Mixed train from Yelverton. When the Tavistock Goods is assisted by a Bank engine in the rear, the wagons must be formed next to the train engine, but when the train is worked by one engine the wagons must be formed next to and in front of the brake van, and the van shunted on to the Princetown Branch line to stand before any other work is performed.
When the latter arrangement is made, the traffic for Princetown will be dealt with as follows :—
The person in charge of Yelverton must take care that no more wagons are put off in the Refuge Siding than can be conveyed by the Mixed train.
When there is traffic to be picked up from the Refuge Siding at Yelverton, the traffic on the train for Princetown must be placed on the Princetown Branch line attached next to the brake van, and the Guard must see that the wagons, together with the brake van, are properly secured by brakes and sprags before detaching the front part, and going back to pick up the traffic in the Refuge Siding. When the latter traffic has been attached to the engine, etc., the wagons must be drawn out of the Siding and propelled with caution against the train standing on the Princetown Branch. The whole of the train except the van must then be set back, traffic for the Princetown Branch must be placed in the Refuge Siding, and, after the van on the Princetown Branch line is attached, the Freight train may proceed on its journey.
A Goods brake van will work from Princetown on the first available train from that station, and the engine of that train must pick up the wagons in the Refuge Siding on arrival at Yelverton and form them in the Mixed train thence.

Working of Through Coaches Plymouth to Princetown.

The following instructions must be observed in dealing with Through Coaches for Princetown which are put off Down trains at Yelverton :—
1.   The coach or coaches must be detached on the Down Loop line at Yelverton, the brake of the coach being put on or vehicle properly secured before it is detached.
2.   The Princetown train must then be backed out from the Branch line, drawn through the Up Loop, and backed to the coach, which must be coupled to the train. The engine must then push the train over the Down Loop until clear of the Branch points, when it can be drawn to the Branch platform or despatched direct, as may be necessary.

HORRABRIDGE.

Horse boxes, carriage trucks, and other vehicles must not be detached at this station, or left on the Main line, unless they are properly secured from running down the incline.

Shunting Freight Trains.

When any shunting is being done at Horrabridge, in connection with a Down Freight train, the points for the Down Shunt Siding must always be set for that Siding, and no wagon or part of a train is to be allowed to stand on the Tavistock side of the Siding points.
On arrival at Horrabridge Station all Up Freight trains must be shunted into the Shunt Siding before being uncoupled to do station work.

PRINCETOWN BRANCH.
Loads on Trains.
The loads on Passenger trains worked by one engine and one Guard on this Branch must not exceed six eight-wheel Passenger vehicles. Owing to the sharp curves the working of six-wheel coaching stock over this Branch is prohibited. Coaching stock exceeding 9 feet 3 inches wide must not work on this Branch.

Wagons loaded with granite must never to sent by Passenger train.

Snow Storms.
When there is a drift of snow in prospect, the engine working on the Princetown Branch, provided there is the opportunity of doing so, must be run to and fro over the threatened spot. The Station Masters at Princetown and Yelverton must direct this to be done according to the end of the Branch at which the engine is at the time. If the use of the snow plough becomes necessary, a telegram to that effect must be sent to the District Traffic Manager and to the Locomotive Foreman at Laira.

Lowry Road Level Crossing near 3¾ mile post, between Burrator and Ingra Tor Halts.
Treadles operating warning bells at the crossing are provided.

Enginemen and Guards must keep a good look-out when approaching and passing this crossing, and in the event of the gates being open to the road or the warning bell not ringing, report accordingly at the next station, where arrangements must be made for the necessary attention to be given. Until the warning bell is again in working order, Drivers of all trains must be instructed at Princetown or Dousland, as the case may be, to bring their train to a stand and satisfy themselves that all is clear, before passing over the crossing.

Drivers of all Up and Down trains must sound the whistle when approaching Lowry Road crossing.

The speed of trains passing over this crossing must not exceed 10 miles per hour.

Swell Tor Siding.
The points at this Siding are locked by key attached to the Train Staff.

All Up Freight trains having to stop at Swell Tor Siding to put off or take on wagons, must be backed into the Siding clear of the Main Line, and the points must then be set normal. All shunting must be done in the Sidings.

All wagons put off at Swell Tor must be placed on the Loop line farthest from the Main line, and all wagons to be taken on must be placed on the Loop nearest the Main line.

Engines are not allowed to go farther than is necessary for shunting purposes at the quarry end of the Loop. Engine Stop Board is provided.

When trains are ready to come out of the Siding, and the points are properly set for the Main line, the Guard must put down sufficient brakes to stop the train as soon as it is clear of the Main line points, and he must ride in the brake van to apply the brakes.

Under no circumstances must Down trains do work at this station. Any empties or wagons of coal for the Siding must first be taken to Princetown, and returned thence by any Up Freight train.

When shunting is finished and the train has been drawn out of the Siding, the points must be set and locked for the Main line.

When it is necessary to supply Swell Tor Siding with empties from Princetown this may be done under Electric Train Staff Regulation 8A, and the engine and van may return from the Siding without going through the Section. When the work is complete the engine can propel the brake van back to Princetown.

Vehicles standing at Princetown.
By day no vehicle must be allowed to stand on the Platform line the station side of the points leading from the Carriage Shed to No. 1 Siding, unless the brakes are properly and fully applied so as to prevent the possibility of the vehicles running away.

By night all vehicles must stand the Princetown side of the points leading to No. 1 Siding, and the points must be turned for that Siding.

Dousland.
All Up trains must stop at Dousland Station.

Excursion Trains to Dousland.
With a view to avoiding the use of two engines on Excursion trains between Yelverton and Dousland, such trains as require assistance between the points named will be timed to reach Yelverton to connect with one of the ordinary trains, and the following instructions must be carried out:—

The ordinary Branch train will be drawn up to the Yelverton Branch Starting Signal. The Excursion train, which must not exceed eight eight-wheel coaches, will then draw ahead in the direction of Horrabridge over the points leading to the Branch line, and be steadily backed on to the Branch train. Both trains will then be coupled together, and when this is done, the combined trains may be started. The Enginemen must carry out the pre-scribed rules, and be careful to start their engines at one and the same time, in the manner described in Rule 133 and in the General Appendix.

On arrival at Dousland, the combined train must be stopped with the coaches of the ordinary Branch train at the platform, and while the passengers are alighting, the Branch train must be uncoupled by the Branch Guard, and as soon as the passengers have alighted, and the Train Staff for the onward section has been handed to the Engine-man, the Branch train will proceed on its journey to Princetown. The Train Staff must be retained by the Engine-man of the Excursion train, which will be slowly propelled to the platform, and when the passengers have alighted, the empty coaches will return to Yelverton after the Staff has been placed in the instrument, and "Line clear" obtained from Yelverton for the empty train with the Train Staff, as usual.

While the Excursion train is standing at Dousland platform, the Loop points must be set for the Loop except when it is necessary to place the level crossing gates across the line to permit vehicles to pass over them.

Loaded Passenger trains may be banked in the rear from Yelverton to Dousland in accordance with the instructions on page 145 of the General Appendix, which must be strictly adhered to. Distance 1 mile 51 chains. Gradient rising all the way. Ruling gradient 1 in 40.

The arrangement outlined above will also apply in the case of empty coaches going to Dousland to work the return Excursions at night.

Princetown Branch—*continued.*
Motor Trolley System of Permanent Way Maintenance.
The instructions on pages 65-68 of the General Appendix apply. The Home Station of the Gang is Princetown.
Telephones and Key Boxes are fixed, as under :—

Group 1 (one key)		Group 2 (one key)			
	m. ch.		m. ch.		m. ch.
Key Box No. 1 .. .. 0 19½		Dousland .. 1 47		Key Box No. 5 .. .. 5 79	
Dousland 1 47		Key Box No. 2 .. 2 73		Key Box No. 6 .. .. 7 1	
		Key Box No. 3 .. 3 63		Key Box No. 7 .. .. 8 3	
		Key Box No. 4 .. 4 71		Key Box No. 8 .. .. 8 73	
				Princetown 10 32	

NOTE.—The telephones communicate with the Signalman at Dousland.

HALTS AT WHICH STAFF IS NOT KEPT.

The following are the halts where staff is not kept, and the supervision of these halts comes under the Station Master at the Station shewn below. The Station Master must visit the halts from time to time, to see that the premises are in proper condition, and that gates, notice boards, shelters, seats, etc., are in order :—

Name of Halt.	Station supervising Halt.
Burrator	Yelverton.
Ingra Tor	Princetown.
King Tor	Princetown.

HALTS, CLEANING, LIGHTING, Etc.

The Engineering Department will see that the Halts and Platforms where no staff are employed are kept clean, and the Platforms sprinkled with sand when necessary. Guards will be held responsible for calling attention to any cases where these places are dirty, or to any unusual circumstance such as damaged lamp glasses, disfigured notice boards, etc.

40

Stations in the Plymouth Division where Engines can take Water—*continued.*

Station.	Where Cranes, etc., are situated.
	Branches.
Yelverton..	Down Platform and Princetown Branch Line.
Princetown	Locomotive Engine Shed.
Horrabridge	Up and Down Platforms.

COUPLING AND UNCOUPLING OF ENGINES OF PASSENGER TRAINS EXCEPT WHERE OTHERWISE SHOWN.

The following arrangements will apply to the coupling and uncoupling of engines in the Plymouth Division.

Station.	Work performed by Fireman.	Work performed by Traffic Department.
Princetown	Arrival and Departure	Shunting.
Yelverton	Main Line and Branch Departure ..	Arrival and Shunting.

Inclines steeper than 1 in 200—*continued.*

Incline situated between	Length of Incline.	Gradient one foot in	Falling towards	Places at which Notice Boards have been fixed and at which trains must stop to put down brakes.	Modifications of or additions to the Standard Instructions for working Inclines.
				Princetown Branch.	
Yelverton and Dousland Station	1½ m.	Max. 40	Yelverton	250 yards the Yelverton side of Dousland Station, 1m. 34ch. Trains pick up brakes at Horrabridge	Freight trains must not descend this incline at a higher speed than 20 miles an hour and must stop dead at the Yelverton Home Signal.
Dousland Station and Lowry Road Level Crossing	2 m.	Max. 41	Dousland	At Lowry Road Crossing, 61 ch.	Freight trains must not descend the incline from Princetown to Dousland at a higher speed than 20 miles an hour.
Lowry Road Level Crossing and 4¼ mile post	¼ m.	Max. 41.	Princetown	—	
4¼ mile post and Princetown	6¼ m.	Max. 41	Yelverton	At Princetown Station, 10 m.	

GROUND FRAMES AND INTERMEDIATE SIDINGS.

Name of Station or Siding.	Where Situated.	By whom Attended.	How Locked.
Dousland	At Station	Signalman or Porter-Signalman	Electrically locked from Signal Box. Standard Key of Cabin kept in Signal Box.
Swell Tor	Between Dousland and Princetown	Guard of Train	Annett's Key on E.T.S. Box locked when not in use by Annett's Key.

WHISTLING AT LEVEL CROSSINGS.

Drivers of all trains must sound their whistles when approaching the following places :—

Where Whistles **must** be sounded.	Position, and whether Whistle Boards provided.
Princetown Branch.	
Dousland Crossing	Between Dousland and Princetown.
Prowses Crossing	,, ,, ,,
Lowry Road Crossing	,, ,, ,,

LIST OF PUBLIC LEVEL CROSSINGS.

Name of Crossing.	Where Situated.		Whether Block Post.	If not a Block Post whether Gatekeeper Indicators, or Bells are provided.	Whether there are signals.	Whether the Gates are interlocked with the Signals.
	Between	And				
Princetown Branch.						
Dousland	Princetown ..	Dousland ..	,,	—	,,	,,
Prowse's ..	,, ..	,, ..	No	Gatekeeper	,,	,,
Lowry Road ..	,, ..	,, ..	,,	Warning Bells provided.	,,	No.

ENGINE TURNTABLES.

Station.	Diameter.	Where situated.
	Ft. In.	
Princetown	23 6	In Engine Shed.
Yelverton	23 6	Near South end of Station (Princetown Branch).

RESTRICTIONS AS TO THE WORKING OF STOCK OVER CERTAIN BRANCH LINES.

Branch.	Restriction.
Princetown	Six-wheeled Coaching Stock must not work over this Branch, nor coaches exceeding 9 ft. 3 ins. over panels at waist.

INSTRUCTIONS AND RESTRICTIONS WITH REGARD TO WORKING OF 70 FOOT STOCK.

Station.	Line over which 70 foot stock must not pass.	Line over which 70 foot stock must pass with caution.
All lines.	**Princetown Branch.**	

STATIONS IN PLYMOUTH DIVISION WHERE RE-RAILING RAMPS ARE KEPT.

Station.	Where stored.
Yelverton	Under stairs, Down Platform.

STATIONS AT WHICH LOOSE SCREW COUPLINGS ARE KEPT—PLYMOUTH DIVISION.

Referring to page 145 of the General Appendix, Emergency Loose Screw Couplings are provided at the following Stations :—

Station.	Number of Couplings.			Station.	Number of Couplings.		
	| Type. |				| Type. |		
	4	5	6		4	5	6
Yelverton	—	1	—				
Princetown..	1	—	—				
Horrabridge	—	1	—				

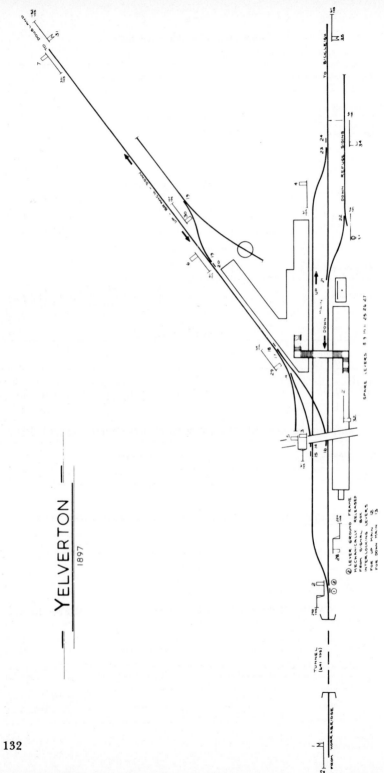

YELVERTON

1897

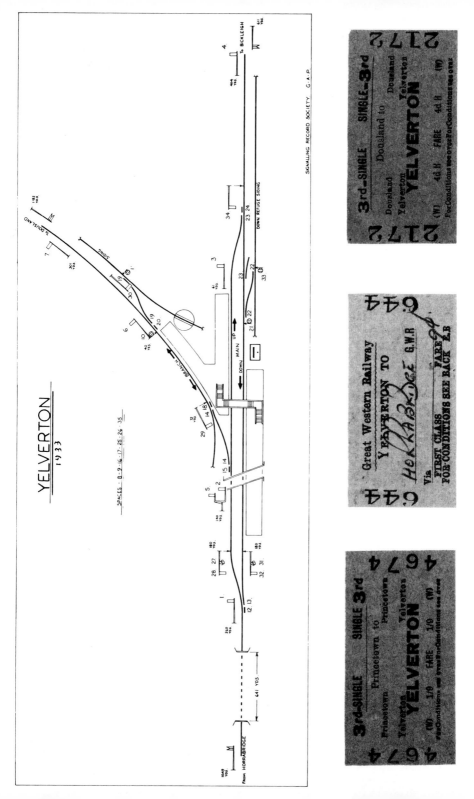

YELVERTON
1933

SPACES - 8-9-16-17-25-26-35

SIGNALLING RECORD SOCIETY G.A.P.

DOUSLAND

OLD BOX

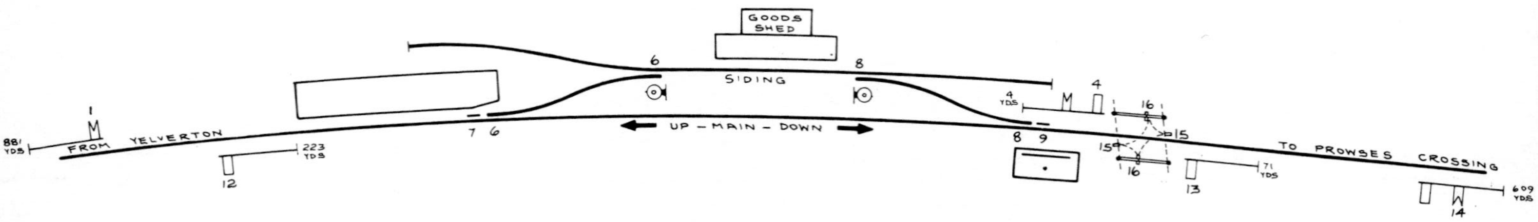

GOODS SHED
SIDING
UP – MAIN – DOWN
FROM YELVERTON
TO PROWSES CROSSING
881 YDS
223 YDS
4 YDS
71 YDS
609 YDS
1
12
7 6
6
8
8 9
4
16
15
13
14

SPARE LEVERS 2.3.5.10.11.
LEVERS 7 & 9 LOCKED BY KEY ON TRAIN STAFF

SIGNALLING RECORD SOCIETY

J.P.M. 12.3.77.

193
Gt Western Ry Gt Western Ry
Dousland Dousland
TO
KING TOR HALT
THIRD CLASS
1/2 C Fare 1/2 C
King Tor King Tor
FOR CONDITIONS SEE BACK W.D
193

489
Gt. Western Ry. Gt. Western Ry.
Princetown Princetown
TO
INGRA TOR HALT
THIRD CLASS
8½d. C. Fare 8½d. C.
Ingra Tor Ingra Tor
FOR CONDITIONS SEE BACK E
489

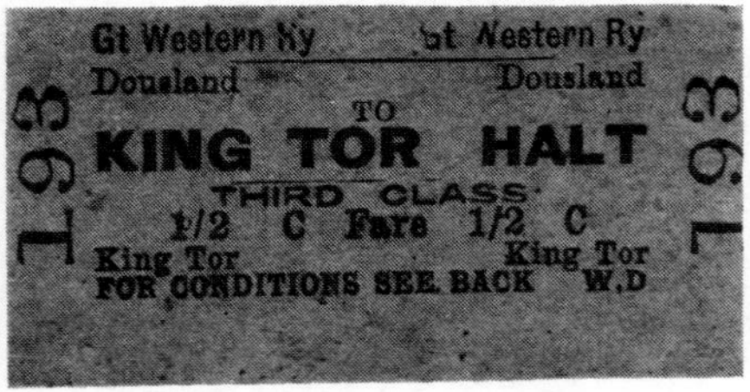

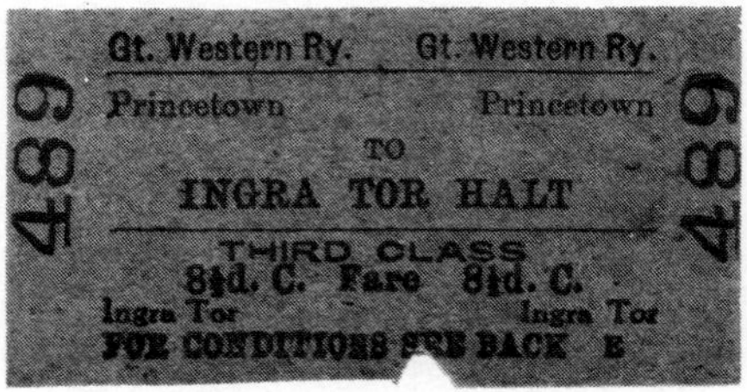

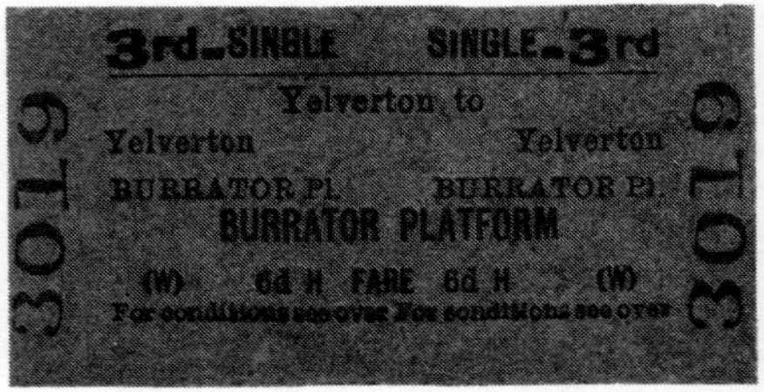

3019
3rd–SINGLE SINGLE–3rd
Yelverton to
Yelverton Yelverton
BURRATOR PL BURRATOR PL
BURRATOR PLATFORM
(W) 6d H FARE 6d H (W)
For conditions see over For conditions see over
3019

— DOUSLAND —

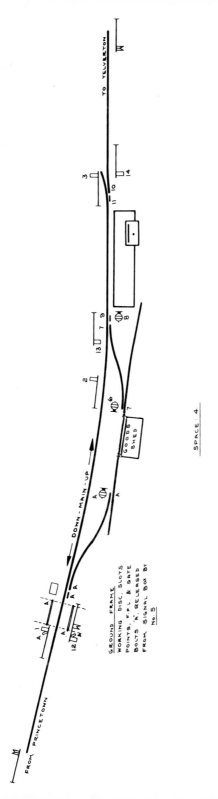

TO YELVERTON

DOWN — MAIN — UP

GOODS
SHED

FROM PRINCETOWN

GROUND FRAME
WORKING DISC. SLOTS
POINTS, F.P.L. & GATE
BOLTS 'A' RELEASED
FROM SIGNAL BOX BY
No. 5

SPACE: 4

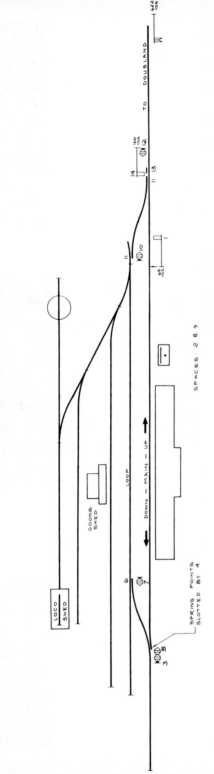

PRINCETOWN

The Dousland to Princetown staff.

A.R.K.

137

PROWSES CROSSING   Late 1890's
Sp.3.

580yds

8yds

30 yds

Dousland

Princetown

538 yds

PROWSES CROSSING ON CLOSURE – 1956

580yds

Dousland

G F

Dousland 'up'

Princetown

533 yds

LOWERY ROAD CROSSING   Late 1890's
Sp 1·4·5

3m 58chs

640 yds

Princetown

Dousland

450 yds

LOWERY ROAD CROSSING ON CLOSURE – 1956
Warning bells operated by treadles

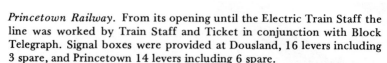

630 yds

Princetown

Dousland

460yds

Princetown Railway. From its opening until the Electric Train Staff the line was worked by Train Staff and Ticket in conjunction with Block Telegraph. Signal boxes were provided at Dousland, 16 levers including 3 spare, and Princetown 14 levers including 6 spare.

Swell Tor siding was laid in and ready for inspection by Board of Trade 20th December, 1883. Inspected 11th January, 1884.

Initially the intermediate sidings were protected by signals and locked by a key on the train staff. After the introduction of the Electric Train Staff the signals at the intermediate sidings and the ones controlled by levers 2 and 3 at Dousland were taken out of use. A new box, Dousland Barn, was ordered in 1914. The box contained a 14 lever frame and was completed on 11th June 1915. The existing box was reduced in status to a ground frame.

EGGWORTHY SIDING 4m 68chs   Sp 1·4

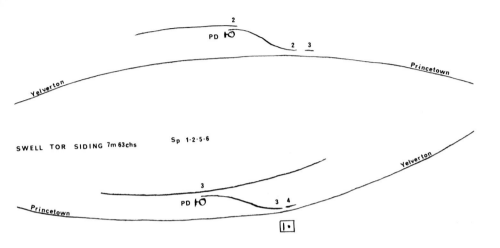

SWELL TOR SIDING 7m 63chs   Sp 1·2·5·6

ROYAL OAK SIDING 8m 75chs

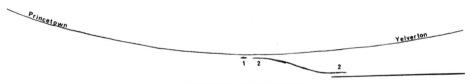

PRINCETOWN - EARLY LAYOUT

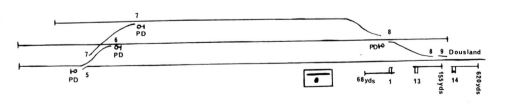

Spare Levers 2·3·4· 10·11·12

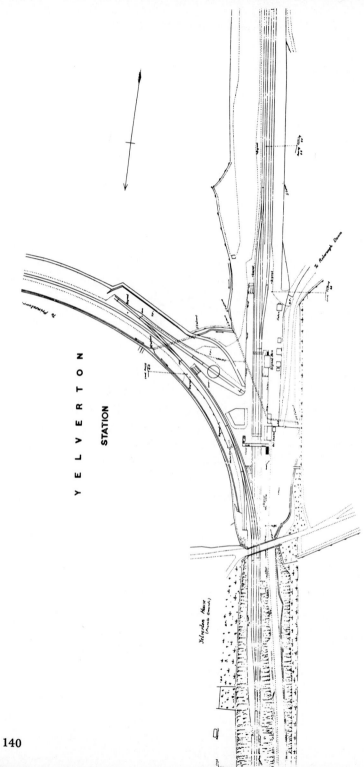

Y E L V E R T O N

STATION

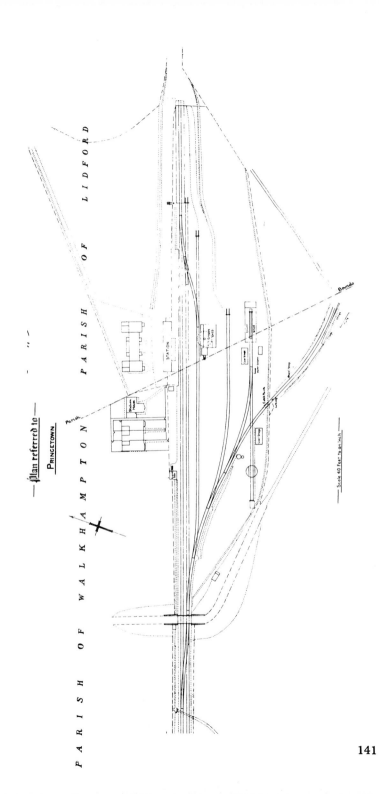

Plan referred to

PRINCETOWN

PARISH OF WALKHAMPTON

PARISH OF LIDFORD

Scale 40 feet to an inch

141

APPENDIX

Memories of some who knew the branch well.
Photographs of surviving items on the Princetown branch today.

Mr J. Brokenshire of Cornwood, former signalman at Princetown during the second world war recalls . . . . .

Snow memories on the branch.
"Older men working on the branch related to me how that, during heavy snow the permanent way staff would stay on duty to assist in getting the engine off the last train of the day away to shed. On one occasion, having completed this task, they joined hands and struggled through very deep snow to the village square, but then having to part and go their separate ways, deemed it too dangerous to proceed and so once more joining hands they returned to the station waiting room where they spent the night."
"My experience of a snowstorm was when the last train of the day ran into a drift at King Tor Halt and Foreman Stephens walked through to Princetown with the 'train staff'. A volunteer was needed to accompany the Foreman when he returned to his train. I filled that role! At first it was feared that the engine was derailed, but later the crew corrected their mistake by using the p.w. phone box further down the line.
A snow plough set out from Laira depot and on arrival came onto the back of the marooned train and hauled it back to Yelverton where refreshments were provided for the passengers and the crew. When on the way back, the train and plough reached Johnsons cutting, the regulator was opened and the engine charged the snowdrift sending huge columns of snow against the bank on either side. Several runs were made at it until it was possible to pass.
The branch train then left Yelverton and arrived at Princetown about seven hours late, at 3 a.m.!"
"A drift once filled the space between the passengers and goods platform, level with the top.
Frost, so severe, would sometimes freeze the oil in the axle boxes and wheels to the line. I have seen waggons being hauled out of the coal siding with their wheels refusing to turn."
"Often during the winter packed ice would form between the running rail and the check on the many curves of the branch. It was thought this, if allowed to remain, might cause a derailment and during very severe weather the length gang would be employed keeping the gap clear with pick axes."

Wartime memories on the branch.
"A special train ran carrying prisoners from 'Camp Hill I.O.W.' to Princetown handcuffed in pairs. They left the train and walked to the prison."

142

"Government stores were mainly for the Royal William Yard, Devonport, an outstation extension of which, was provided by erecting numerous Nissen huts on prison ground at Princetown during the war years."

"A direct telephone line from Princtown to Plymouth was installed during the war years, prior to this all telephone messages were taken to be transmitted by the signalman at Yelverton."

Other memories.

"Certain trains known as 'mixed trains' were permitted on the branch. These were often loaded to the hilt and meant such a struggle for the little engine. The toughest section seemed to be on the curves between Ingra Tor Halt and Yes Tor bottom."

"You could walk the distance between the track at Yes Tor bottom and King Tor Halt in the time it took the train to go around Swell Tor and King Tor and up to the halt."

"A pony fair was held annually on the first Wednesday in September. On that day a special train would be at Princetown. Most times it rained and young ponies in the pens would be tummy deep in mud which meant that drovers would be knee deep! The Station Master was always pleased to welcome an official from Plymouth to supervise the loading and deal with any claims for compensation that might arise."

"Prisoners just released and being accompanied by a warder to the station, would travel on the early morning train. By their mis-shapen forms, it was easy to see that the authorities had 'turned a blind eye' to the fact that they were concealing some precious possession about their person. It was possibly something that they had made whilst inside, and it was their furtive manner that gave them away. I have often said that few people have been to prison as often as I! I used to go monthly to collect the account owing to the railway, often less than £1."

"Guard Frank Prowse moved from Falmouth to Princetown and at the time swore that he would not stay in such a climate for any longer than necessary. He came to love Dartmoor however, and he spent the rest of his life there. It was his suggestion that 'Royal Oak' was changed to 'King Tor Halt'."

"A case of tickets was carried in the guards van and the guard would issue tickets to passengers joining the train at the various halts."

"Mr Hansford Worth lived at Princetown during the war. He travelled to Plymouth daily, returning on the tea time train, where upon his wife never failed to meet him with a kiss in return for a posy of flowers which he always brought for her."

(Note:— R. Hansford Worth was a civil engineer and a great authority on Dartmoor.)

"The original intention was to construct the line right into the village square, hence the reason for naming the Inn, 'The Railway Hotel'. It has now been renamed 'The Devils Elbow'."

Workings.

"On bank holidays, a number of the Plymouth relief staff would be stationed at Burrator Halt to collect tickets from passengers alighting there. This was discontinued during the war years."

"At Swell Tor ground frame, one was not supposed to leave the train on the main line whilst the engine called at the sidings to pick up any granite traffic. The spur however was not sufficiently long to accommodate more than a few waggons."

"The last train that called was for the purpose of transporting derelict crane, purchased from the quarry owners, to H.M. Dockyard."

"One railway employee I knew would busy himself between trains with ferret and nets, gun and snares! This occupation augmented his meagre income somewhat. One day a 'very well to do' gentleman expressed interest in his hobby and the said employee showed him how it was all done, allowing his visitor to fix most of the snares himself. That night, several rabbits were caught by other means and furtively placed in the snares. The next day they both met again and revisited the sites of the snares and the visitor expressed his amazement and his thanks with a very handsome gratuity!"

"An Annetts key on the train staff used between Dousland and Princetown was able to operate the ground frame at Swell Tor Quarry sidings, which were served by 'up' trains only."

"A signalman's extraneous duties at Princetown were trimming, cleaning and refilling signal and station lamps. He also had to deal with all incoming goods traffic and accounts, and assist with all general station duties."

"At Dousland the signalman would go to the level crossing ground frame when he heard the train approaching from the Princetown direction and open the gates. He would close them again behind the train, following it on foot for the short distance past the goods siding and shelter, and would then despatch the train to Yelverton."

"On sheep fair days, once yearly on the first Tuesday in September, sheep would be put on rail by their scores at Dousland."

Mr Victor Thompson, veteran passenger, recalls. . . . .

TWELVE MONTHS STRETCH ON THE PRISON LINE

"The 1 in 8 gradient of Peak Hill sweeps up and away from Dousland and people into five miles of wilderness; in winter, five miles of noisy dark with the distant glimmer of Princetown above Devil's Bridge. The prospect could disconcert a motorist. The boy with the push-bike, the week-day orphan, lodging and working in Plymouth, fixed his eyes on the lights and headed out for a brief reunion with his 'prison' family. It was a regular weekly trek whatever the season, as long as the saddle bag held oilskins and a puncture outfit. Train tickets, even in the 'thirties, were luxuries on fifteen bob a week.

I could never get to the railway bridge at the foot of Peak without being overcome by the gradient, by the nearness of the last evening train out of Yelverton. She would bore out of the woods above Burrator to take the moorland climb and for a moment the road would flicker with bright cuts of light, till the November night swallowed her up above Walkhampton. I'd be left with the soft-sharp smell of steam, forced down by the drizzle and five miles still hazing up into horizons as black as the moor. Long before I reached Princetown, Driver Gough would have bedded down the 2-6-2, ash-pan emptied, shed locked for the week-end. By the time I'd shunted off oilskins, Bill would be pulling off double twenties for starters down in the Prison Officers' bar.

Throughout the 'thirties, for me the railway was something of a rainbow with me at one or the other end of it and never a pot of gold until '46 when I took to being a schoolmaster down along Walkhampton with a season ticket from Princetown.

Commuting on the Prison line had all the privileges of a club. The 7.30 pulled out with a single coach and corner seats for most of us; folks with jobs in Tavistock and pupils at the Grammar School; warders on day leave with wives for Plymouth shopping. Two teams of men worked the line. Bill Gough came down, how many years back, from Old Smokey and looked as though he belonged to the tors. He'd take a stand close to the station gate with an eye on the approach road hemmed on one side by cattle pens, draughty enough in winter, but filled to the top rails one day in the year for the pony fair. Any straggler from 7.29 on would be jolted into a gallop. The whole thing, in winter, took on a Sinai touch when the commandments issued from billows of steam blotting out the platform. But Bill never lost a man. There was one touch-and-go moment when I nearly broke his record; on a morning of snow down to three feet — in the better places — and lungs morticed to my ribs. The tail lamps reddened the end of the platform gliding off towards King Tor, when the signalman waggled the distant in a sort of, 'Did you forget something?' And back it all came to pick up the lost sheep. The sort of chivalry you associated with the Great Western crest.

The occasional stranger on the 7.30 was a time-served man, the only one on the train with a one-way ticket. One of the warders would be there, looking like someone you thought you knew in civvies. This escort was just as far as the station's single platform and there was instant agreement, automatic, unspoken to leave one compartment reserved, out of compassion. To give him time to take it all in, the sense of an old debt paid, the freedom, the light off the moor.

King Tor was the first halt, a gaunt wooden deck as barren as the moor, standing on stilts up to its knees in heather. Miles away, a shimmer marked the quarries at Merrivale where an old friend worked as a boy, 'for a penny an hour, cutting stone for General Buller's statue up Exeter way'. An iron sign warned travellers to keep a dog on a lead for fear of snakes. Not that anyone ever turned up, with or without dog and you wondered what founded the ritual of a morning stop. Two minutes silence, maybe, for all Napoleon's men who died in building Princetown? It was dismal enough in wintry times to raise the ghost of

Conan Doyle's hound of the Baskervilles. There was one dog at least in the village which lollopped away in wide wailing circles rather than follow its master through the old hut circles showing up like bones from old peat.

From here the line looped around in descent to Ingra Tor, once a miniature quarry with its own tiny siding still there, rusting with silence. You could listen to a skylark lost in a glare of sunrise before clattering on down to that bridge at the foot of Peak Hill to see Spring-new lambs or Winter-old memories. Sometimes, a boy with a bike.

Above the dam at Burrator, someone had built another wooden halt for Sheepstor folk, a mile or so along the road which crossed the granite wall across the Meavy. The whistle drowned itself in all that water, not even a ripple left to disturb the village or the three white Rajah Brookes at the head of the churchyard. There was an endless murmur of the water-fall which, as summer drew out, grew quieter and you looked for that church spire to pierce the lake. And it never did. Nothing but the peak of Sheepstor, upside down and in perfect symmetry.

Dousland was the end of the week-day line for me and a walk downhill to the village school; a droop uphill to the 5-20 at the end of the day. Except one day; the day of the Dartmoor run cab-side. Driver Gough took bye-laws seriously. I was stacked back against the coal bunker just in case the Chairman happened to be this way and to keep me out of the fire.

There was a quarry just below Sharpitor with a permanent resident — an old red fox. Throughout summer it derided the train daily, turning its back on the whistle with one ear cocked for any further insults. Not that Bill hated animals for just above Princetown he made note of a ram with its horns hopelessly mixed with the wire fence. I was used to meanderings but taken aback to be told that GWR brass decreed a halt to all traffic while drivers untangled the mess. All part and parcel of the Dartmoor haul, where timetables gave way to man or beast along its narrow — but not so straight — path.

The course was not always smooth.

Down at Yelverton before each return trip, the single empty coach was backed up the incline, braked and slipped and the loco switched into a siding just long enough for it. Points re-set, the coach ran downhill to the platform and the loco switched out again to run down and couple up at the proper end. This arrival among friends, for every passenger was, could make a driver forget that the points were still open to the siding. With his engine up-ended down the bank, thrown clear of the cab, Bill remembered too late and a startled signalman left the Tavvy traffic to itself to snap it up on record.

Snowfall was dramatic. The road from Yelverton to Plymouth could be dry while the Princetown branch lay under six-foot drifts. On the climb up to Ingra the train would back down for a one-two-three — charge through billows of snow along either window. Late-comers from Tavvy once made the Yelverton change-over into a bus which surrendered at Peak Hill and slid back to hastily made hotel beds at the junction. All at the Company's expense.

Even down there on the fringe of the moor, the freezing silence drove my bride and I from a honeymoon hotel in '48 into the friendly warmth and bustle of the Princetown train — the whole coach to ourselves — and we spent the rest of the week by the family fireside. Relatives poured up from Plymouth on the Saturday train for a surprise party and must have put a bewildering peak on receipts for February that year.

Rolling stock doubled on the good days, holidays, fair days, every Saturday. Mecca for the outlanders was Plymouth shops, pasties on the Hoe, Argyle and the pictures. Only one of the last two, for curfew was 6 pm for the last train out of Millbay to cross Union Street bridge, city lights marking a mile-long fairway up to Stonehouse, jabbing you with a sense of being sent off to bed just as the party began. Through North Road and Laira the lights stayed with you, though in more domestic clusters, till you came out between the clay-white glimmer of the Plym and the old tramway falling off Lee Moor. The Exeter line parted, swinging off right as you went to Marsh Mills and high above blackberry lanes to Plymbridge. One late summer evening, years away, three friends and I and each of us eight, grabbed purple-stained bags, trying to cope with broadening cramps and lengthening shadows and a certainty that no train would ever pass this way again. With one brief toot, like the one we heard that night and told each other we knew it would come, we left them behind to bore into tunnels of trees to Bickleigh and Shaugh then the silent, wide mistiness of the Meavy.

Yelverton was a surge of shadows and voices, up over the footbridge by gas-light. Back in the Tavistock train, people changed over to corner-seats, staring out at the Princetown crowd and wondering, no doubt, what they had to be cheerful about. They pulled out for Horrabridge and late tea at 'Tavvy' while we filled the compartments with bargains from Spooners and Groucho Marx gags. There was no-one but the man in the box to see us leave, heading out for the tors and the wind gibbering in the wires, where an old red fox deep in a winter den would not prick an ear at our passing, at it all passing."

Mr G. F. Jakeman of Wakefield, Yorkshire recalls . . . . .
"I was a regular traveller on the train from September 1939 to April 1946 whilst at school in Tavistock and whilst working in Plymouth. As I remember the train departed from Princetown at 7.35 am, 10 am, 12.30 pm, 4 pm and 6 pm. It arrived back at Princetown at 9.30 am, 12 noon, 3.30 pm, 5.30 pm and 7.40 pm. Until the early 1940s there was an additional service on a Saturday which arrived in Princetown at 10.30 pm. There were four scheduled stops between Yelverton and Princetown namely Dousland, Burrator, Ingra Tor and King Tor. The latter three were Halts and were nothing more than platforms of sleepers. Dousland was staffed by booking clerk cum porter but the Halts were not staffed.

Princetown station was a single platform on which was a booking office, a waiting room and toilets. There was also a signal box detached from the station. It was painted fawn and brown and the design was as

147

for the majority of GWR stations. It was staffed by a Station Master, signalman and porters.

Station personnel lived in the village as did the men who manned the train. They were all part and parcel of the village. Listed below are some of the staff:

        Jack Mount — Engine driver
        Bill Gough — Engine driver
        Frank Prowse — Guard
(Father) Charlie Windsor — Station Master
(Son)   Charlie Windsor — Station Master
        Albert Stevens — Fireman

The village including the prison depended a great deal on the railway both for transport of people and transport of goods.

When prisoners were released from the prison they were escorted to the station by an officer and seen off at 7.30 am. Prisoners under escort were also conveyed by train to Princetown. The longest train I ever saw on that line was in about 1941. The train consisted of two engines and six carriages and it was used to bring the prisoners of Parkhurst to Dartmoor. Prisoners were chained together and were marched from the station at Princetown to the prison. It must have been one of the biggest movement of prisoners organised by The Prison Commission.

Goods brought to the village by rail were until the early 1940s taken from the station by horse and wagon and delivered to consignee. The man who had the contract for this service was Jim Crocker and he was also the landlord of the Plume of Feathers Inn which was an old coaching inn. Not until about 1942/43 did Jim buy a petrol driven lorry and it was about that time The Royal William Victualling Yard set up a sub depot in Princetown using Blackabrook House and Nissen huts erected close by. This sub depot existed as such until after the war.

The railway was very much part of the village and some events which in the '40s were taken for granted are now amusing.

It was not uncommon for a child to be late arriving at the station to catch the 7.35 am. If the train had left but not passed the arch about 150 yards outside the station the Station Master would often use his whistle to recall the train so that a late arrival could board.

It was also not unusual for the train to stop anywhere along the line between Dousland and Princetown to pick someone up. Many times I was picked up complete with ferret and dog.

Whist drives were a common feature of village life and the train drivers were two regulars at the drives. Passengers on the train always knew when Jack Mount was driving and when he wanted to get home a few minutes early in order to go to a whist drive. He used to have the throttle well open and the train really rattled along. The wheels of the carriage grated hard on the additional rail around the sharp bends. I don't remember ever being late or even on time on 'whist evening'."

Two recent views of the site of Lowery Crossing. a) The grass strewn trackbed looking back towards Burrator. b) The filled cutting through the conifer woods looking towards Peek Hill.   *4.3.78 A.R.K.*

Princetown station. a) Looking eastwards in the hazy sunshine on 4th March 1978.
b) Looking westwards on 16th January 1977, under threatening snow clouds. A
solitary G.W.R. 'Private Path' sign stands outlined against the wintry sky. *A.R.K.*

HISTORICAL NOTES.

Yelverton. The crossing place was ready in time for the arrival of the L. & S.W.R. narrow gauge trains. The layout consisted of up and down loop lines controlled by a distant, home and starting signals in each direction; all signals being of the semaphore type. The up points were 180 yards from the box, the down points 177 yards. As the maximum distance for working points was 150 yards the Inspecting Officer suggested either a box was provided at each end of the Crossing Place or the points must be worked from ground levers interlocked with the box. To overcome the problem a ground frame was provided adjacent to the points by the tunnel and the other points were moved nearer the box.

When the Princetown line was being constructed one of the conditions was, either better facilities were provided at Horrabridge or a new station would be required at Yelverton. The latter was adopted but when the new station was inspected by the Board of Trade it was found that the common rail had not been altered on the down platform. This meant that narrow gauge trains were about two feet from the platform edge. The layout was corrected before the station opened. The additional points and signals were connected to the existing box. The box now had 20 working levers and 4 spare.

A lot of new work was undertaken in 1897/98. The down platform was extended from the overbridge towards the tunnel. The up platform was widened and as the up loop line was now nearer to the down loop line it meant a slight alteration to the junction with the Princetown line. At the same time the loop lines were extended towards Plymouth and a new signal box displaced the existing box. The new work was completed on 11th February, 1898 and inspected by the B.O.T. on 30th March, 1898.

The famous snake notice, recovered and restored by members of the Plymouth Railway Circle and now residing in a local museum at Saltram House, Plymouth.

A.R.K.

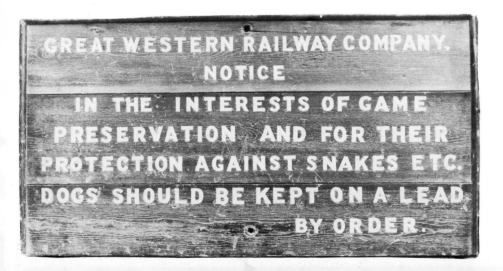

GREAT WESTERN RAILWAY COMPANY.

NOTICE

IN THE INTERESTS OF GAME PRESERVATION AND FOR THEIR PROTECTION AGAINST SNAKES ETC. DOGS SHOULD BE KEPT ON A LEAD.

BY ORDER.

The Author, photographed here with his wife Marjorie.

There can be few people more well known in local railway 'circles' than Tony Kingdom.

Born in Plymouth in 1931, the son of the late Engr. Comdr. Charles M.S. Kingdom, himself a steam engineer with the Royal Navy from 1906 until 1934, Tony became interested in steam at a very early age and still vividly recalls 'interviews' with the driver and fireman at the start and, often again, at the completion of a train journey during the 1930's. Similarly, he also has vivid memories of trainspotting at Plymouth Laira, North Road and Mutley during the war-time years and seeing many locomotives and rolling stock 'foreign' to the area.

With the demise of the steam era in the early 1960's, Tony turned his attentions towards the field of preservation, and the many activities that followed included being Chairman of the South-West Group of the Great Western Society from 1968 until 1972 and a founder member of the Dart Valley Railway Association.

Pressure of work and the responsibilities of a young family ultimately weaned Tony away from preservation work during the early 1970's, but the vacuum was to be immediately filled by him becoming an author of Railway books. This, in turn, subsequently led to the successful publication of no less than seven titles between 1974 and 1982, while in 1990 the lack of the publisher did nothing to prevent the appearance of his eighth book: using the name ARK Publications, he published it himself!

Tony, now retired after a long career in the Post Office Engineering Dept. (now British Telecom), in which he graduated to the position of Engineering Training Manager, Westward District, currently lives in Newton Ferrers with his wife Marjorie. He has two grown-up children, Roger and Nicola, and three young grandchildren, and enjoys gardening, is a keen photographer and, during the summer months, looks forward to boating and caravanning with his wife. In addition, he likes to spend any spare time researching the history and experiences of the Second World War and, looking to the future, hopes to produce further works on Westcountry Railways as well as seeing some more of his out-of-print titles republished, this being the first.

Other books by A.R. Kingdom:

The Yealmpton Branch	OPC	1974
The Railways of Devon	Bradford Barton	1974
The Great Western at the Turn of the Century	OPC	1976
The Ashburton Branch	OPC	1977
The Princetown Branch	OPC	1979
The Newton Abbot Blitz	OPC	1979
The Turnchapel Branch	OPC	1982
The Plymouth Tavistock and Launceston Railway	ARK Publications	1990